COOPERATION
BETWEEN
TYPES OF LIBRARIES
1940-1968

COOPERATION BETWEEN TYPES OF LIBRARIES 1940-1968

An Annotated Bibliography

RALPH H. STENSTROM
*Library Research Center
University of Illinois
for
The Illinois State Library*

CHICAGO
American Library Association
1970

The study reported here was made at the
Library Research Center, University of Illinois,
through a grant from the
Illinois State Library.

International Standard Book Number 0-8389-0094-1 (1970)

Library of Congress Catalog Card Number 71-140212

Copyright © 1970 by the American Library Association and
the Illinois State Library

All rights reserved. No part of this publication
may be reproduced in any form without permission in
writing from the publisher, except by a reviewer who
may quote brief passages in a review.

Printed in the United States of America

CONTENTS

Preface — vii

Introduction — 1

Scope of the Bibliography — 1

Types of Libraries — 1

Search Strategy — 2

Arrangement of the Annotated Bibliography, Appendix, and Indexes — 4

Review of the Literature — 6

Annotated Bibliography — 19

Appendix — 133

Author-Project-Organization Index — 143

Types of Cooperative Activity Index — 151

Types of Library Cooperation Index — 158

PREFACE

In 1966 the Library Services and Construction Act was amended to include three additional titles as part of the federal government's support of library service. The new Title III, "Interlibrary Cooperation," provides funds to states which had submitted and had approved "plans for establishing and maintaining local, regional, state or interstate cooperative networks of libraries." In order to qualify for approval the plans had to "provide policies and objectives for the systematic and effective coordination of the resources of school, public, academic, and special libraries and special information centers for improved services of a supplementary nature to the special clientele served by each type of library or center."[1]

Thus, for the first time, federal funds became available to the states specifically for the planning and implementation of programs involving different types of libraries and information centers. A number of projects have been approved and begun under the provisions of the act and planning for many others continues.

The literature on cooperation is extensive and varied in both content and quality. Pleas for cooperation abound in the journals as do descriptions of the "how we do it" variety. Titles assigned to articles frequently tell little about the content, and indexing is not always specific enough to identify the kinds of activities or libraries involved. The result is that a search for articles on specific kinds of cooperative activities requires sifting through masses of material, much of which is inapplicable. This bibliography should help to identify material of interest to people planning cooperative activities. Brief annotations provide some indication of the nature of the projects and the types of libraries involved.

This bibliography, based primarily on a search of *Library Literature,* was not intended to be complete. Some worthwhile cooperative projects

1. "Library Services and Construction Act Amendments of 1966," Public Law 89-511, approved 19 July 1966.

may have escaped notice, and undoubtedly projects exist which have not been described in the literature. Omissions are regretted, and users of the bibliography are requested to send information to the Library Research Center, University of Illinois at Urbana.

The compilation of this bibliography represents the work of a number of people in the Library Research Center. The original suggestion that a bibliography on this subject would be helpful came from Dr. Herbert Goldhor, Director of the University of Illinois Graduate School of Library Science. The work on the project was begun by Galen Rike, formerly a Research Associate of the Center, assisted by Irma Kosa, Elaine Albright, and Susan Roumm. Together they completed most of the literature search and prepared annotations for many of the earlier publications. After Mr. Rike's departure, work on the project was resumed under the direction of the present editor with the assistance of Robert McCown and Charlyn Costello. Numerous suggestions and general direction of the project were supplied by Dr. Terence Crowley, Director of the Research Center. Helpful assistance was provided by Mrs. Sandra Overman, Mrs. Rosa Wood, and Miss Nanette Bensyl, who did much of the preliminary typing, and Mrs. La Verne Caroline, Secretary of the Research Center, who directed preparation of the final copy.

I would like also to acknowledge the help given by the *ALA Bulletin, College and Research Library News, Library Journal, Special Libraries,* and *Wilson Library Bulletin* in printing the request for information on this topic and thank the many people who responded by sending descriptive materials on a variety of cooperative projects.

Ralph H. Stenstrom

Introduction

SCOPE OF THE BIBLIOGRAPHY

Period covered. The period covered by this bibliography is 1940-1968. A few items published in 1969 have been included, but no systematic search of the literature of that year was made.

Subject coverage. Two criteria governed the selection of items for inclusion in the bibliography. The first was that the material deal with cooperation involving more than one type of library; the second was that the description be of a program in actual operation. This second requirement has not been enforced for some projects still in the proposal stage, when they seemed likely to be implemented or when they contained information of value to other planners. Also, a number of the proposals and plans were the result of the work of librarians from different types of libraries and, in themselves, represent a form of the kind of cooperation under discussion here.

Material describing projects in foreign countries has been included when it was published in English.

TYPES OF LIBRARIES

This bibliography uses the traditional typology of libraries as its starting point—public, school, academic-research, and special libraries. This classification is most commonly used and provides a sufficiently clear distinction for the purposes of this work.

Public libraries are those which are free to all residents of the library's district and supported primarily from general public funds or taxes levied for library purposes. Local public libraries, systems of public libraries, and state library agencies are included in this category.

School libraries are those maintained by the governing boards of schools whether they be public, private, or parochial. School libraries at the elementary, junior high school, and senior high school level are included.

Academic-research libraries include the libraries of institutions of higher education, both public and private, as well as libraries which, while they might be defined as either public or special, are widely known for their research resources. Junior college libraries, college libraries, university libraries, and technical school libraries are included as academic libraries. The Library of Congress, the Newberry Library, and Linda Hall Library are examples of nonacademic research libraries.

Special libraries are those directed toward making information available to people within a particular organization with fairly well-defined information needs. Business and industrial libraries and the libraries of nonprofit organizations are common examples.

While distinctions between research and special libraries are not always easily made, it is felt that in the case of this bibliography, no serious problems are created.

SEARCH STRATEGY

In 1955, John Rather published a bibliographical essay on library cooperation in which he reviewed the literature on examples of all types of cooperation using *Library Literature* as the basis for his search.[2] In order to extend the period covered by the present bibliography and to facilitate the search for the earlier items, Rather's bibliography was used as a starting point. All items in the Rather bibliography were read to see if they contained examples of cooperation between different types of libraries. All pertinent articles in the Rather bibliography have been included here, thus providing coverage for the period 1940-1954.

For the period from 1955 through 1968, *Library Literature* was searched under the same headings searched by Rather. These were:

Acquisitions, Cooperative
Bibliographical centers
Cataloging, Cooperative
Catalogs—Union
Cooperation
County libraries
Interlibrary loan
Library extension
Public libraries—services to
   colleges and universities

2. John Rather, "Library Cooperation: A Bibliographical Essay Prepared for the California State Library and the California Library Association," *California Librarian* 16:299-310 (Oct. 1955).

Public libraries—services
   to schools
Regional libraries
Storage and deposit libraries.

To this basic list of readings the following new headings were added and searched:

Interlibrary relationships
Networks of libraries
School and public library relationships.

Since Rather's bibliography was supplemented by Speed's bibliography[3] of items on cooperation in the field of audiovisual materials, the latter was also searched for items which involved different types of libraries. Those which applied have been included and this subject area updated by searching *Library Literature* 1955-1968 under the following headings used by Speed:

Audiovisual materials
Microfilm
Motion pictures
Phonograph recordings
Photo lending procedures
Picture collections.

On the chance that many instances of cooperation may never have been described in the literature, an announcement requesting descriptions of such programs was placed in the *ALA Bulletin, College and Research Libraries News, Library Journal, Special Libraries,* and *Wilson Library Bulletin* in the summer of 1969. This announcement elicited numerous responses, some accompanied by descriptive brochures and pamphlets. Those items which met the criteria for inclusion have been listed, although in some instances they are virtually unobtainable except from the cooperating libraries.

There are a number of limitations to the search strategy the user should be aware of. The search was limited, basically, to *Library Literature,* and only articles published in English have been included. Thorough coverage of monographic works dealing in part with interlibrary cooperation cannot be claimed. Annual reports of libraries and governmental agencies have not been cited except when they were brought to our attention or were immediately available. Newspaper accounts, press

   3. William J. Speed, "Library Cooperation in the Field of Audio-Visual Materials," *California Librarian* 16:311-12 (Oct. 1955).

releases, staff bulletins, and descriptive brochures have not been included unless they were sent in response to the request for information. An additional limitation is that citations in the articles were not systematically searched.

While many librarians cooperated by sending information on cooperative projects, the response cannot be considered to be complete or even representative. Time did not permit a follow-up in cases where information supplied was incomplete.

A more comprehensive search would have included a number of other indexes, direct requests to state and federal library agencies, or direct contact with individual libraries. The bibliography is far from being a complete inventory of interlibrary cooperative projects or a complete listing of the pertinent sources of information. For items listed in *Library Literature* for the period covered, complete coverage has been attempted.

ARRANGEMENT OF THE
ANNOTATED BIBLIOGRAPHY, APPENDIX, AND INDEXES

The entries in the Annotated Bibliography are arranged chronologically, first by year, then by season or month, to enable users interested in the most recent developments to turn directly to such entries. Monographic works are listed alphabetically by author at the beginning of each year's listings. This chronological arrangement permits the user to trace the development of a particular project over a period of time during which there may have been several articles on that project.

The Appendix contains items that were received in response to the request for information printed in the professional journals. Many of these answers came in letter form and could not easily be fitted into the format of the bibliography. The numbering of these appendix entries is continued from the main body of the bibliography.

Three indexes have been prepared to provide different kinds of access to the material listed. The first is an author-project-organization index (p.143) which includes the names of authors of articles and monographs and the titles of organizations and cooperative projects.

The second index (p.151) is a classified index of the types of activity described and uses the following eight categories listed by Purdy in his description of the interrelations among public, school, and academic libraries:[4]

Union catalogs and lists
Cooperative development of resources
Sharing resources in terms of use

4. G. Flint Purdy, "Interrelations among Public, School, and Academic Libraries," *Library Quarterly* 39:52-63 (Jan. 1969).

Communication
Centralized processing
Cooperatively sponsored planning and surveys
Cooperative storage
Cooperative computer center.

A more complete description of the specific activities included under each of these headings is provided when necessary in the index. Articles dealing with activities in more than one of these areas are listed under all of the categories that apply.

The third index (p.158–59) is arranged by types of libraries involved in the cooperative projects. Thus there is a heading for Public-Academic Libraries followed by a listing of the entries describing projects involving these two types of libraries and so forth for each of the possible combinations of libraries. The number of entries under some of the headings, e.g., School-Special Libraries, is relatively small. On the other hand the number of articles describing School-Public Library cooperation is so large that this heading has been omitted from the index. It was felt that perusal of the bibliography itself would reveal these items as quickly as listing them in the index.

Review of the Literature

The objective here has been to compile the literature relating to cooperation between different types of libraries rather than to make any systematic analysis of the kinds of cooperation in process or the types of Libraries followed by a listing of the entries describing projects involving general way some of the types of cooperative activities that are most common, the kinds of libraries that are involved, and any trends which are discernible.

The identification of efforts which can be regarded as truly cooperative is not always easy, as Esterquest has pointed out.[5] Some of the entries included in this work describe programs of service in which libraries interact, but in which there is no mutual exchange of services or materials. The provision of classroom collections to schools by the public library or centralized cataloging provided by a state library agency are frequently cited as examples of cooperation, but in fact involve only the provision of a service by one library agency to another. Other examples exist where services are provided, but where no exchange of services takes place.

Another problem which has been cited and which continues is that much of the literature on cooperation consists of poorly written accounts of very local and limited programs. Such reporting inflates the literature without adding substance to our knowledge of the nature of cooperation, the problems involved, or the solutions of those problems.

One other very serious limitation of the literature on cooperative programs is the lack of evaluation. Few failures are analyzed and reported, and little is said of the extent to which existing programs are achieving

5. Ralph T. Esterquest, "Cooperation in Library Services," *Library Quarterly* 31:71-89 (Jan. 1961).

the objectives set for them. There is some indication that projects sponsored by state and federal funds will generate more evaluative reports and help fill this very important need.

Since the quality of the literature on cooperation varies greatly, one of the shortcomings of an annotated bibliography, as Rather has suggested, is that all items tend to appear to have equal value.[6] This problem is further complicated by the fact that it is impossible in many instances to make any judgments about the worth or success of projects as they are reported in the literature. No attempt has been made in this bibliography to evaluate the activities described, but a few items which seem to have very broad applications or which contain novel features have been singled out.

One thing which is apparent from a review of the literature on this subject is that it is increasing rapidly. The number of articles written since 1960 is greater than the output of the previous 20 years. The most dramatic increase has come since 1966, the year of the addition of Title III to the Library Services and Construction Act. Although many projects operate without federal funds, the impact of the new legislation is unmistakable.

Since the entries generally are restricted to examples of working cooperative projects, the Annotated Bibliography does not fully describe activities which are in the planning stage, nor does it provide the perspective of what the total plans are for library development in some states. Plans and proposals have been included where they seem likely to be implemented in part in the near future, but even these do not tell the complete story of the direction in which library development is moving. Readers may want to refer to the bibliographies of Bunge,[7] Rike,[8] and the ERIC Clearinghouse for Library and Information Sciences[9] on statewide surveys and plans for a broader look at library development, and for the perspective in which interlibrary cooperation is developing. Library agencies in a number of states are either working at or planning for the creation of statewide networks which will link all types of libraries to the total resources of those states.

There are also other forms of interlibrary cooperation which are not

6. John Rather, "Library Cooperation: A Bibliographical Essay . . .," *California Librarian* 6:300 (Oct. 1955).

7. Charles A. Bunge, "Statewide Public Library Surveys and Plans, 1944-1964," *ALA Bulletin* 59:364-74 (May 1965).

8. Galen E. Rike, *Statewide Library Surveys and Development Plans: An Annotated Bibliography, 1956-1967* (Research Series no.14 [Springfield, Ill.:Illinois State Library, 1968]). 105p.

9. ERIC Clearinghouse for Library and Information Sciences, *Library Surveys and Development Plans: An Annotated Bibliography* (Bibliography Series, no.3 [Minneapolis: Sept. 1969]). 43p.

adequately reflected in the literature. Some of these are long-established forms of cooperation which are taken for granted. Interlibrary lending is accepted as standard practice and frequently crosses the line between different types of libraries. The trend recently, however, has been toward the formalization of channels to be followed in this area. The compilation of union lists has been a common type of activity involving different types of libraries, and remains a common starting point for other cooperative activities. The literature reported here also says little of the many informal cooperative arrangements which have grown up between libraries over the years. School and public libraries have frequently worked together out of necessity; academic and public libraries have cooperated by sharing resources and by opening their facilities to each other's clientele; public and special libraries have often worked together in supplying each other's specialized and general needs; these and many other kinds of cooperation have been common practice and frequently go unnoted in the literature.

Some programs such as the Farmington Plan, the United States Book Exchange, the Duplicates Exchange Union, and various others sponsored or supported in large part by the Library of Congress are well known and descriptions of them are easily accessible in the literature; these have probably not received their full share of attention in this bibliography.

With these reservations in mind, an attempt will be made to review briefly some of the cooperative programs involving different types of libraries. Numbers in parentheses refer to items describing the project mentioned in the Annotated Bibliography.

Academic-Public-Special-School. While a good deal of attention is presently being paid to the concept of statewide or regional networks which would link all types of libraries and make the resources of large areas accessible, there is little indication from the literature cited here of widespread implementation of this kind of program. A number of programs sponsored jointly by academic, public, and special libraries are in operation, but there are few which include all four types of libraries. Parts of the explanation of this fact may rest with school libraries, which do not fit easily into cooperative programs with academic and special libraries. School library needs are fairly distinct, and the collections they build are rarely of value to the users of academic and special libraries. Activities involving all four types of libraries are limited for the most part to the compilation of union lists or participation in planning councils.

The most prominent move toward the involvement of all libraries in cooperative programs is exemplified by the statewide library development plans being pursued in a number of states—among them, New York, Pennsylvania, and Illinois. Although the basis for these programs is the formation of public library systems, there are efforts to involve other types of libraries, particularly academic and special, in a multilevel system of resources and services. Local public libraries have access to resources at the district or system level, and these centers in turn have access to major resource centers at academic, large public, state, and, in some cases, special libraries. In New York the systems are supplemented by reference and research agencies which provide more specialized information needs. While the move toward the establishment of this kind of program is gaining momentum, there are still unanswered questions about how the school libraries fit into such plans. Are school libraries to have direct access to the resources of district centers and other backup sources, or are students at grade and high school levels expected to gain access through their public libraries? There is also the possibility of the development of parallel school library networks which will establish direct contact with other regional or statewide networks.

Perhaps answers to some of these questions will be provided by the Indiana Libraries Study. This investigation of information needs and available resources was planned and conducted with reference to all types of libraries and information centers in the state. The last two phases of the study are concerned with the development of recommendations and their implementation through legislation. An advisory committee of two people representing each of the four types of libraries plus two trustees is working with the project staff.[10]

Academic-Public-Special. Cooperative programs among these three types of libraries are more common than those involving all four types of libraries and have increased rapidly since 1966. Earlier programs in this country were commonly associated with the compilation of union lists, joint contributions to union catalogs and bibliographic centers, and participation in storage or deposit centers. One of the more formal arrangements is the Library Group of Southwestern Connecticut which includes public and industrial libraries and the University of Connecticut in an arrangement of planning and sharing of resources (199).

England has had a longer history of formal cooperation among academic, public, and special libraries. These three types of libraries have worked together within the framework of England's regional system in which academic and special libraries have contributed information to

10. Peter Hiatt. "Indiana Libraries Study," *Focus on Indiana Libraries* 22:135-38, 140 (Sept. 1968).

the regional union catalogs, have taken responsibility for building collections in specialized areas, and have made materials available for interlibrary lending. In addition, a number of organizations composed of these three types of libraries, centered usually around a public or academic library, have been created to improve access to specialized information needs (162, 167, 177, 231).

In the United States the number of programs has increased rapidly since 1966, due in part to the availability of state and federal funds from Title III of the Library Services and Construction Act and the State Technical Services Act. One of the most comprehensive programs is under development in New York City as part of the state's system of reference and research agencies. The New York Metropolitan Reference and Research Library Agency, Inc. (METRO) is the result of a long period of cooperative planning by public, academic, and special libraries. METRO attempts to improve reference and research service in the New York metropolitan area by facilitating the use of present resources and developing additional resources. Cooperative acquisitions, retention of last copies, an information transmission network, interlibrary delivery service, and centralized storage are some of the programs in operation or under consideration (246, 249, 253, 270, 308, 328).

Other cooperative projects involving these three types of libraries include New York's pilot interlibrary loan experiment (NYSILL, 290, 315) in which the state library has contracted with libraries to act as backstop centers for interlibrary loan requests, the Greater Louisville Technical Referral Center (363), the Rochester Regional Research Library Council (344), proposed cooperation in the Washington, D.C., area (295, 337), and an increasing number of teletype networks tying the resources of these kinds of libraries together. Indications are that the number of cooperative projects of this kind will continue to increase.

Academic-School-Public. Most of the items in this category describe efforts of public and academic libraries to help meet the needs of students at the high school level. The relationship of the public library to the schools has a long history and will be discussed later. The role of the academic library is usually that of acting as a backstop source for the public library. Some academic libraries will permit high school students to use their facilities and resources, but usually with some restrictions, and only after all other sources have been exhausted.

Some proposals have been made for coordinating the resources of these three types of libraries (30, 191), and recently there have been some attempts to establish working relationships. The Scarborough Information Network (SIN, 332) links the branches of the public library with the library's Administration Center to speed the delivery of needed materials to the branches. The Centennial College of Applied Arts and Technology has joined the communication system, and recently one high school has elected to take part. In Wisconsin, the Northeast Wisconsin Intertype Libraries (NEWILL, 383) includes all three types of libraries in an organization which is exploring a number of areas where cooperation is considered possible. A union list of periodicals has been compiled, and means for sharing resources are being investigated. The Southern Oregon Library Federation includes a large number of libraries—academic, public, and school—and the federation has recently established the position of coordinator to direct cooperative activities among the member libraries (285).

The number of such projects is still small, indicating perhaps some difficulty in establishing programs which will be of mutual advantage to academic, school, and public libraries.

Academic-Public. Several different patterns of cooperative arrangements exist between academic and public libraries. Where communities have both academic and public libraries, the nature of the cooperation is determined in part by the relative size and strength of the libraries. Where one of the two is considerably stronger, it is usually a matter of the stronger supplementing the resources of the weaker through interlibrary loans or by allowing direct use of its facilities and collections. The Peoria (Ill.) Public Library permits students of Bradley University and Illinois Central College to borrow from its collections without charge (310, 348). In other instances this service is extended on payment of a fee, either by the student or by the academic institution (27).

In cases where libraries are of nearly equal strength, or when they have specialized collections, other opportunities for cooperation exist. The North Texas Regional Library, consisting of both academic and public libraries, has produced a union list of serials and has reached agreement on some cooperative acquisitions programs (7, 20, 35). The Farmington Plan, although principally for academic and research libraries, includes a few large public libraries; it is an example of cooperative acquisitions on a national level (41); other well-known plans include those of the Detroit Public Library and Wayne State University (125, 148), the St. Louis Public Library and Washington University (186), and the long-standing agreements among Chicago's public and private research libraries. In Great Britain the University of Durham and a number of public libraries maintain a joint reserve stock of fiction, and in the East Midlands academic and public libraries cooperate in the provision of foreign language materials (101). Germany has a project in which twelve academic and public libraries work together to rebuild collections badly damaged by the war (113), while in France academic libraries place heavy reliance on the public libraries for materials confiscated during the Revolution (188).

Cooperative acquisitions programs imply the need for the exchange of information about holdings and arrangements for sharing their use. The exchange of catalog cards, contribution of information to union catalogs or bibliographic centers, and the compilation of union lists are commonly used means of exchanging information about holdings. A number of communities have liberalized policies on interlibrary lending, and a number of more recent developments have speeded the communication of information and the delivery of materials. Teletype networks are becoming more and more common; facsimile transmission, while still experimental, is under consideration; wide area telephone service, wide use of inexpensive photocopies, and delivery service are being increasingly used to facilitate the exchange of information and materials. A number of these programs are sponsored by groups of libraries or are coordinated by one of the participating libraries. The Southeastern New York Library Resources Council provides member libraries with delivery service, photocopies, telephone credit cards, and a union list of serials (339). The MINITEX experiment, sponsored by the University of Minnesota Library, is a teletype network connecting a number of academic and public libraries in the state; the aim of the experiment is to collect cost data on supplying the information needs of these libraries and to determine whether such a program is feasible (274, 346).

An additional feature of academic-public library cooperation has been mentioned earlier. This is the role which academic libraries frequently play as backstop or resource centers in statewide plans for the development of public library systems. Most of these plans include some form of compensation to the cooperating libraries in return for attempting to fill interlibrary loan requests which cannot be met by local, district, or state library agencies.

Recent developments indicate increased involvement on the part of public and academic libraries as state and federal funds are used to compensate libraries which provide service outside their usual patron group.

Academic-Special. The number of articles describing cooperative agreements between academic and special libraries is not particularly large, and it is possible that many informal agreements exist which have not been described in the literature. Among the activities described, the most common are the exchange of catalog cards, cooperative acquisitions, participation in storage libraries and bibliographical centers, compilation of union lists, and, in a few cases, the transfer of collections to libraries with special strengths in the given subject area.

More recently there have been a number of more formal programs instituted which stress the role of the university library in helping to provide service to industry. A study conducted by the Claremont Colleges and industrial firms in the area suggests the possibility of a joint science library to serve both groups by using highly automated record keeping and search procedures (203).

One of the more comprehensive and well developed schemes is the Regional Information and Communication Exchange (RICE) located at Rice University. Industrial firms are invited to tap the resources of a number of academic and special libraries along the gulf coast from Louisiana to Mexico. Firms may approach the Exchange directly or by using the teletype facilities of one of the libraries in the network. Industrial firms may either elect to pay fees based on use or take out annual memberships in the Exchange (202, 233, 266, 267, 286).

Similar programs of service to industry have been instituted at the California Institute of Technology (286), Stanford University (208), Massachusetts Institute of Technology (286), the University of Wisconsin (252), and Southern Methodist University (251). Representative services include on-site use, interlibrary loans, and photocopy service, as well as bibliographical searches in some cases.

A novel experiment is the Pennsylvania Technical Assistance Program, a mobile service to industry. Patterned after traditional bookmobile service, PENNTAP's van visits industrial firms with materials most likely to be of help in meeting industry's information needs (345).

If funds continue to be available, more plans involving academic libraries with special libraries and industry should continue to develop.

Public-Special. A large proportion of the articles in this category deal with programs in England where cooperation between public and special libraries is common and quite formalized. The Sheffield Interchange Organization (SINTO, 44, 102), and the Cooperative Industrial and Commercial Reference and Information Service (CICRIS, 120, 146) are just two of the large number of organizations which work to pool the resources of public and industrial libraries.

In the United States, as with academic-special library cooperation, there are probably a large number of informal arrangements between special and public libraries which are not cited in the literature. One arrangement which is cited is the Denver Public Library's cooperation with the Colorado Scientific Society and the professional engineers of the state. These groups gave their libraries to the Denver Public Library and contribute annual payments for the purchase of materials in the areas of their interests (33).

Other examples include service to industry by public libraries, as in Detroit (33); reliance of public libraries on special libraries, particularly in such special subjects as local history and medicine; and service to state institutions, such as hospitals, by public libraries.

School-Public. The similarity in the collections and patrons of school and public libraries is reflected in the large volume of literature describing school-public library cooperation. For a major part of this century schools relied heavily on the public library to provide both instructional and supplementary reading materials. Classroom collections, deposit collections, bookmobile visits, and administrative supervision were services commonly provided by public libraries during a time when school libraries were either nonexistent or very poorly developed. This pattern of service remains in some areas, but, more generally, school libraries have improved to the point where they provide the greater portion of the instructional materials. There is still heavy reliance on the public library in most cases for supplementary instructional materials and for general and recreational reading.

A number of school boards continue to contract with public libraries for school library service. A common pattern is for the school board to provide physical quarters, staff, and funds for materials and for the public library to do the ordering and processing of materials and occasionally to provide general administrative supervision.

The "combination" library, i.e., a public library branch housed in a school and giving service to both students and the public, was considered for some time to be an economical and efficient means of providing both school library service and service to adults. The advantages and disadvantages of this arrangement are still argued from time to time, but it is generally conceded that in such situations service to adults invariably suffers. The "combination" library is seldom recommended today and examples of it are much less common (32). A modified form of this plan is used in some communities during the summer months when school libraries, usually in areas where there are no branches of the public library, are used as branches of the public library. The service is provided jointly by the public library and the schools and is aimed, for the most part, at school aged children. There is some discussion of having schools provide year-round library service, but as yet there is no indication that this has become widespread practice.

At the present time service arrangements between school and public libraries are much more likely to be based on specific contracts and limited to specific functions. Centralized processing is an example of a service frequently provided on this basis. A number of public libraries provide this service to schools on a per book rate; some examples are given also of joint processing centers for school and public libraries. Large scale processing arrangements exist in Hawaii where processing for all school and public libraries is done at one center (319), and in Georgia where the state provides catalog cards to public and school libraries (12, 28, 116, 131).

There are some arrangements between school and public libraries in the areas of cooperative selection and ordering, but these tend to be much less formal. They are more likely to consist of joint book review and discussion meetings than specific assignment of responsibility for collecting in specific areas.

By far the greatest number of cooperative programs between these two types of libraries involves informal agreements worked out between the librarians and confined to the local communities. Many of these programs have been established in response to problems arising from students' use of the public library. Advance notice of class assignments, multiple paperback copies of heavily used titles, special reserve shelves for student materials, and consultations with teachers are commonly used procedures to meet student needs.

Even more common are class tours of the public library, instruction in the use of libraries, book talks to classes and PTAs, summer reading programs, and varying degrees of cooperation in book selection.

Despite the large number of reports on school-public library cooperation, there are indications that in many states the respective roles of the two libraries remain confused and that few firm policies exist to guide cooperative programs. One survey (277) reports that in some places school-public library cooperation is discouraged.

Some recent developments suggest some new directions in which school libraries might go, either separately, or in conjunction with public libraries. Several Title III projects have included surveys of students' needs and opinions on library service (195, 212). These surveys have usually been a part of the planning for cooperative projects between school and public libraries, and are among the few attempts to utilize the experience and opinion of students in formulating policy. A comprehensive survey of student needs and public and school library resources is underway, financed by the Bureau of Research in the Office of Education.

A second development, still in the experimental stage in some cases, is the creation of the position of liaison librarian or school-public library relations consultant. In the past public library staff members have been assigned such duties on a part-time basis, but now there is a move toward official recognition of the need for such a person and establishment of separate staff positions. The duties of the liaison librarian are to discover student and teacher needs and to coordinate the efforts of teachers and library staff, both school and public, in meeting these needs (214, 232, 235, 261, 305).

A third development involves the creation of school library networks similar in organization to those for public libraries. Such networks would work toward the pooling of resources; the building of union catalogs; and the centralization of technical processes, delivery service, and related library services. An eventual working relationship between these networks and others which exist for public, academic, and special libraries offers the possibility of greatly expanded resources for school libraries (234).

Other. There are four other possible combinations of libraries, all of them involving school libraries: public-school-special; school-special; academic-school; and academic-school-special. These combinations rarely appear in cooperative projects. Of the entries listed, only three describe programs involving public, school, and special libraries. The first of these is an area union list which includes periodical holdings of some high school libraries (244); the second is a library council which includes all types of libraries in meetings to discuss mutual problems (355); and the third is an informal local arrangement in which agreements have been reached on referral of patrons, interlibrary loans, and acquisitions (365).

Only one item refers to direct cooperation between special and school libraries (286). This article tells of two instances in which special libraries permit use of their collections by high school students. In one case, students have made very little use of the resources, and there is some question of the value of the program. Both programs are one-sided arrangements in which the school libraries offer nothing in exchange for the service given them.

The school library's relationship with the academic libraries is similar to its relationship with special libraries. Some academic libraries permit high school students to use their resources, usually on a restricted basis and with the understanding that the students must exhaust all other sources first (362, 368). This practice is probably fairly common and is not unusual enough to warrant repeated descriptions in the literature. As with the school's arrangements with special libraries, this is also a unilateral program based on the academic library's willingness to extend service to students without payment or any kind of exchange of services.

It is not surprising that school libraries have little involvement with special or academic libraries beyond the rather limited one-way arrangements described. The school library's resources are usually limited and designed to meet rather specific student needs. The material is rarely specialized, facilities are not open to people other than students, and there is very little that the school library has to offer beyond the instructional and supplementary reading needs of students. It is unlikely that the school library will develop extensive reciprocal arrangements with any other than public or other school libraries.

Summary. The preceding review of the literature on interlibrary cooperation is brief and based entirely on the literature cited in this bibliography; it presents only a partial picture of the development of cooperative activities between different kinds of libraries. Nonetheless, it does serve to point out a few of the important developments which have occurred and which seem likely to continue. One is that the amount of cooperation between different types of libraries is not only increasing, but it has done so at a rapid rate since 1965. Another development is that, while many informal agreements of long standing continue to govern cooperation, the trend seems to be toward more formal arrangements, directed in many cases by permanent committees or councils. Interlibrary loan and communication channels are more clearly delineated; positions such as school-public library relations consultant are becoming full-time permanent staff positions; and regional councils are assuming a more important place in planning for cooperation.

The advances of the 1960s demonstrate the importance of outside funding in making cooperative ventures possible. The obstacles created by inadequate funds, the basis of more than just one library's reluctance to participate in joint efforts, have been removed in many instances. While outside funding has been of immense value in the initiation of cooperative programs, to some extent it also changes the nature of the programs developed; rather than being true cooperative projects, many of the programs become services provided by a central agency that are made available to those who express an interest or need. The importance of this fact may be only to demonstrate the importance of adequate funding in reducing the risk involved to those considering cooperative programs.

One shortcoming of this review of the literature, and in part this is due to the literature itself, is its failure to provide the reasons for opposition to cooperative programs or the factors which contribute to their success or failure. Much more evaluative research is needed, and more cooperative programs need to be designed with a built-in evaluative feature. Only then will increasingly effective cooperative interlibrary programs be developed.

Annotated Bibliography

1940

1. American Library Association. "Cooperative Cataloging Committee, Annual Report, 1940," *ALA Bulletin* 34: 579 (15 Sept. 1940).

The Cooperative Cataloging Committee continued to produce cards for monographs in series and foreign books in 1939 with the aid of the General Education Board, the Library of Congress, and 50 cooperating libraries. The General Education Board agreed to extend the time for the use of its grant until 31 December 1941. At the Cincinnati conference the Committee held an open meeting for a discussion of the future of cooperative cataloging. Opinions were given by the university, public, and subscribing libraries. Archibald MacLeish explained the position of the Library of Congress and expressed his interest in seeing the work continued on an equitable basis.

1941

2. Joint Committee of the National Education Association and the American Library Association. *Schools and Public Libraries Working Together in School Library Service*. Washington, D.C.: National Education Assn., 1941.

Working relationships between school and public libraries in ten communities are described. Information is included on the community, the public library, the school organization, the extent and nature of existing school library service, the cost of the program, and the devices and relationships which typify school-public library cooperation. The communities included are Madison (Wis.), Cleveland (Ohio), Harrisburg (Pa.), Cass County (Ind.), Hunterdon County (N.J.), Fairbault (Minn.),

Beatrice (Neb.), Albany (N.Y.), Long Beach (Calif.), and Scotia (N.Y.). Suggestions for improving school-public library relations are given.

3. Govan, Gilbert E., and Rowell, Adelaide C. "The Chattanooga Library Building," *Library Journal* 66: 543-47 (15 June 1941).

The Chattanooga Public Library and the University of Chattanooga Library share the same building, specially constructed to house the two libraries. While entirely separate administratively, the two libraries are so planned that there can be an immediate interchange of services or books. Loans are freely made from one library to another. A union catalog is already being planned. Consultation is frequent over the purchase of books and periodicals to avoid unnecessary duplication.

The combined strengths of the two collections have already attracted other cooperative enterprises. The Chattanooga and Hamilton County Medical Association has joined in the development of a medical library maintained jointly by the public library and the medical association, the books and periodicals of which are available to both the public and the doctors.

The public library, the university, the junior and senior high schools, and the private preparatory schools have organized and are adminstering a cooperative film library.

1942

4. Colorado College and Head Librarians Conference. Special Committee on Centralized Technical Processes and Book Buying. "First Report." Fort Collins: Colorado State College Library, 1942. Mimeographed.

This is the first of three statements from the head librarians of Colorado's academic and public libraries dealing with possible cooperation in technical processing. A study was proposed which would investigate whether centralized technical processing would result in financial savings, greater efficiency in preparation, and better bibliographical control.

This report outlines the steps to be followed in the study.

5. Colorado College and Head Librarians Conference. Special Committee on Centralized Technical Processes and Book Buying. "Planning Studies on Centralization; An Introduction by the Committee to its 'First Report'." Fort Collins: Colorado State College Library, 1942. Mimeographed.

This statement by the Special Committee provides additional explanation of the purposes of its first report. It deals with the question of whether the study should be limited to Colorado or whether it should contain some comparison with similar libraries in other states.

The form of the report and a summary of the comments of various librarians to whom the plan was shown are discussed.

1943

6. Colorado College and Head Librarians Conference. Special Committee on Centralized Technical Processes and Book Buying. "Second Report." Fort Collins: Colorado State College Library, Feb. 1943. Mimeographed.

In this report is expressed the intent of the Special Committee to appoint subcommittees to carry out the study of centralized processing and to initiate programs to solve local problems discovered in library service in Colorado. It is hoped that solutions discovered would be applicable to similar situations in other parts of the country.

7. Kuhlman, August F. "The North Texas Regional Libraries." Nashville: Peabody Pr., 1943. Mimeographed.

The author made a survey of the libraries of Southern Methodist University, North Texas State Teachers College, Texas Christian University, Texas State College for Women, and the public libraries of Fort Worth and Dallas to investigate the areas where cooperation would be profitable and practicable. He suggests that Dallas Public Library and Southern Methodist University Library divide responsibility for economic and business materials, and that they work to avoid duplicate efforts in the purchase and processing of serials. He also urges a similar arrangement for Fort Worth Public Library and Texas Christian University to avoid unnecessary duplication in periodicals and expensive materials.

Ten proposals are offered in connection with the formation of a North Texas Regional Library, among them the recommendation that the North Texas libraries be organized into a system headed by a coordinator of library resources and services for an experimental three-year period. Cooperative efforts should include a union list of serials in the libraries and the expansion of present serial holdings through shared purchasing. Other proposals deal with strengthening collections of other types of materials, the possibility of a union catalog, and financing for the project.

8. Halvorson, Homer. "Library Cooperation in Illinois," *Illinois Libraries* 25: 59-62 (Jan. 1943).

Halvorson suggests that library cooperation was just beginning in Illinois in the early 1940s. The experiences of cooperative ventures such as union catalogs in Philadelphia and Great Britain are cited as examples for Illinois to follow in the future.

9. "Union Catalog Aids Small Libraries," *Library Journal* 63: 950 (15 Nov. 1943).

The Nassau County Library Association (public libraries and two college libraries), maintains a union catalog of holdings at the Valley Stream Free Library on Long Island. Requests for interlibrary loans are made through the Valley Stream Free Library.

1944

10. Carlson, William H. and Smith, Bernice S. "Proceedings of the Conference on Library Specialization," *Pacific Northwest Library Association Quarterly* 8: 52-59 (Jan. 1944).

This is a report of the discussions of the Committee on Bibliography of the Pacific Northwest Library Association. Forty-eight librarians representing 30 libraries in the region took part in the discussions. The main topic was the need for more subject specialization in order to build strong subject collections in the region.

To promote the regional cooperative development of book resources the librarians agreed:

- That participation in the program would in no way restrict any library from purchases in any subject field whatsoever
- That when two libraries decide to specialize in the same subject field the librarians concerned would confer with each other in order to develop their holdings cooperatively
- Libraries would lend books to one another
- Subjects selected for specialization would include fields of particular interest to the life and activities of the Pacific Northwest
- That the Pacific Northwest Bibliographic Center would act as a clearing house for the program, and that each cooperating library would report, once a year, the progress that it had made in its selected field, as well as any new subject specialization it had undertaken.

11. Richards, John S. "Regional Discards of Public Libraries." *Pacific Northwest Library Association Quarterly* 9: 15-18 (Oct. 1944).

Richards proposes that the Pacific Northwest Bibliographic Center take the lead in preparing and coordinating a regional plan for discarding materials and retaining last copies. Each library would assume responsibility for an area in which discards are common and would accept and preserve discards from other libraries.

1945

12. Hubbard, C. S. "Central Cataloging Being Tried," *Library Journal* 70: 310 (April 1945).

C. S. Hubbard, Director of the Division of Textbooks and Library Service of the Georgia State Department of Education, issued a letter stating that, at the request of the Georgia Library Association, the State Department of Education is now prepared to offer state cataloging service to public and school libraries. The service includes catalog cards furnished at a cost of 5¢ per book for all books purchased with school and public library state funds. Each set will include uniformly reproduced cards for shelflist, author, title, and subjects. Manuals will also accompany the cards. Sarah Jones, assistant director, stated that 168 school and 35 public libraries have requested the service as of 5 February 1945.

13. Hodgson, James G. "An Experiment in Cooperation: The Colorado Program of Studies on Joint Action," *College and Research Libraries* 6, no.4, pt. 2: 423-28 (Sept. 1945).

Colorado librarians, including those from state institutions of higher education, private colleges and universities, and the Denver Public Library, "wanted to see if by working together they could improve the library service." The Colorado College and Head Librarians Conference (librarians who were members of the Bibliographical Center for Research—Rocky Mountain Region) elected a "Special Committee for Centralized Technical Processes and Bookbuying" to study cooperation. This committee called a meeting in Chicago in February 1943 "which resulted in the creation of the Joint Committee for the Study of Basic Problems in Technical Processes, whose function was to serve as an advisory clearinghouse for any studies which might be done either in Colorado or in other places." Then a Colorado Special Committee on Studying the Technical Processes was established. This new committee compiled a *Union List of Periodicals Currently Received in the College and University Libraries of Colorado and Wyoming* (Denver Public Library included). A careful analysis of this list was made and reported on in this article.

1946

14. Winslow, Amy. "Library Co-ordination and Consolidation in Metropolitan Areas," in Carleton B. Joeckel, ed., *Library Extension: Problems and Solutions,* p.140-59. Chicago: Univ. of Chicago Pr., 1946.

Amy Winslow reports on some efforts to promote cooperation between libraries in metropolitan areas. The Metropolitan Library Council of Chicago, consisting of 25 members from all types of libraries, is considering a plan for service to areas without libraries, a union catalog, a regional bibliographic center, a storage library, and an interlibrary loan system. Philadelphia's Metropolitan Library Council is studying subject specialization, cooperative cataloging, cooperative technical processing, storage of little used materials, and borrowing privileges. In the West, consideration is being given to having libraries in California, Nevada, and western Arizona join the Denver and Seattle bibliographic centers.

15. Burr, Elizabeth. "The Public Library's Contribution to the Public School," *Illinois Libraries* 28: 64-66 (Jan. 1946).

The contract between the Public Library Board and the Board of Education in Evanston is discussed. The two share the cost of books and salaries for the elementary school libraries. The supervisor of work for children in the public library also supervises the elementary school libraries.

16. Might, Mamie. "The School and the Library Join Hands," *Wilson Library Bulletin* 20: 430-31 (Feb. 1946).

In the Kansas City (Kans.) Public Library the children's librarian visits the schools twice a year for storytelling and the display of new books. The public library sponsors a vacation reading club to ensure that children continue to read during the summer holidays. For parts of the city not near a branch library, the public library lends books to the teachers who, in turn, lend them to the children. The supervisor of arts in the schools selects the students' best works for display in the public library.

17. Joint Committee on Cooperation with Schools. "Better Library Service for the Youth of New Jersey; a Report on Cooperation with Schools, Appointed by the New Jersey Library Association, and the Children's Section of the New Jersey Library Association, March, 1945," *New Jersey Library Bulletin* 14: 147-65 (Spring 1946).

The responsibility of a Joint Committee on Cooperation with schools was to determine the basic educational and reading needs of children and youth which could be met through library service both in and out of school and to suggest ways and means of meeting these needs.

The committee realized that no basic overall plan would suit every community, so three separate plans for cooperation between school and public libraries were drawn up—one each for large, medium-sized, and small communities. The suggestions made by the committee are based largely on examples of already existing types of cooperation between school and public libraries in other areas.

An appendix contains sample contracts drawn up by the committee between boards of education and public library boards.

18. Brunette, Margaret. "A Public Librarian Reports Her Experiences with School Libraries," *Canadian Library Association Bulletin* 2: 77-79 (April 1946).

A description is given of the contract between the Vancouver Public Library and the Vancouver School Board for service to elementary schools. The school board pays for staff, books, equipment, and supplies; the public library provides central quarters and general library facilities. The Schools Department of the public library houses the central pool collection from which the schools borrow, acts as general coordinating center, and is the headquarters for advice and aid in book selection and library procedure.

The public library classifies, catalogs, and prepares for circulation all books ordered for the school libraries. All the school library books are treated as part of one library collection.

A committee consisting of four elementary school librarians, two public librarians, the inspector and supervisors of primary and special class work, together with a high school representative meets monthly. The committee decides general policy, particularly in matters of book selection.

19. Haviland, Virginia. "From Library to School; An Experiment in Cooperation," *Library Journal* 71: 814 (1 June 1946).

Pathfinders News is a three-page bulletin of library and school news, published in Boston. The school children write articles, book reports, editorials, and letters to the editors. Teachers encourage the students and often send in especially good work by the students. The Children's Librarian of Boston Public Library helps in the selection of material for publication. She also records the honor roll of those children who have read and reported on more than eight books.

20. Bailey, Lois. "The Cooperative Program of the North Texas Regional Libraries," *News Notes, Bulletin of the Texas Library Association* 22: 7-9 (July 1946).

The author discusses Dr. A. F. Kuhlman's survey (*see* item no.7) to investigate the possibilities of cooperation between North Texas College and Dallas and Fort Worth public libraries. A summary of Kuhlman's recommendations is included.

1947

21. Downs, Robert B. "Opportunities for Library Cooperation and Coordination in the Richmond Area: Report of a Survey with Recommendations." Urbana, Ill.: The Author, 1947. 17*l.* Mimeographed.

After a survey of library facilities in the Richmond (Va.) area, Downs recommends the establishment of a regional bibliographic center, specialization in acquisitions and the publication of a detailed guide to individual libraries. Ten other recommendations deal with a central storage warehouse, a central bindery, central photographic service, an audio-visual aids center, central processing, a review of policies on newspaper and public documents, delivery service, and in-service training.

22. Kerr, G. "Film Service as a Part of Library Service," *Ontario Library Review* 31: 292-96 (Aug. 1947).

Kerr presents a discussion of the growing awareness in Canadian libraries of the possibilities of films as an educational medium. The National Film Society's activities have become an integral part of Canada's library movement. The Canadian Library Association is a corporate member of the National Film Society and the Film Society is a member of the Canadian Library Association.

The Film Society provides member libraries with deposit collections of films. In East Ontario, Queen's University serves as a film distribution point for libraries and other deposit stations.

23. Branham, Irene. "Serving Children in a Large County," *ALA Bulletin* 41: 439-41 (Nov. 1947).

Kern County Library in California gives service to county schools. The children's book collection is coordinated with that of the school department to avoid duplication. Other schools pay the county library an annual amount of at least $50 per teacher in return for service by the county library. All but the largest schools have joined this service. The money paid by the schools is used to buy supplementary texts, unit materials, maps, globes, and the like. County bookmobiles visit rural schools where teachers and students borrow books.

24. Holden, Edna. "Public Library Service to County Schools," *Library Occurrent* 15: 699-700 (Dec. 1947).

The Logansport (Ind.) Public Library scheduled bookmobile visits to public schools in Cass County to make material directly available to school children and to teachers. Additional deposits of supplementary reading were made to the schools for classroom use during the entire school year.

1948

25. "Library Cooperation in Metropolitan New York; Report of a Meeting of New York City Librarians." New York: The Participants, 1948. 32p. Mimeographed.

This is an account of a working meeting on library cooperation in New York City held 24 February 1948 at the New York Public Library. The discussions at the meetings covered a number of topics. One of the areas in which cooperation might take place was technical services, e.g., a union catalog, cooperative acquisitions, cooperative cataloging, cooperative disposal of duplicates, cooperative binding, and photographic reproduction. The question of providing a regional storage center was also discussed. Another topic was the relationship of undergraduate college students to the public libraries and the question of the difference between a research library and a popular reference library. Various types of libraries (special, law, and others), reported on their feelings toward library cooperation. The report provides a historical prelude to the present METRO System.

26. Brown, H. P. "Alberta Film Pool and Circulating Film Exchange," *Canadian Library Association Bulletin* 4: 99 (Feb. 1948).

Brown describes the program set up by the University of Alberta through its Department of Extension. Films are circulated throughout the area with most of the film libraries being operated by the public libraries. The University of Alberta is the central repository for the National Film Board and the National Film Society whose collections include many films from industrial and governmental sources.

27. "Two Public Libraries Explain Working Arrangements with Colleges," *Library Journal* 73: 179-80. (1 Feb. 1948).

Olean Public Library (N. Y.) serves students and staff of St. Bonaventure College without charge, while Osterhout Free Library serves the students of Wilkes College (Wilkes-Barre, Pa.) for a monthly fee of $150 from the college.

28. Drewry, Virginia. "Centralized Cataloging Frees Georgia's Librarians," *Library Journal* 73: 382-83 (1 March 1948).

Centralized cataloging became a part of the state aid program for libraries in Georgia in the fall of 1944. The Georgia State Centralized Catalog Card Service is under joint sponsorship of the State Department of Education, Textbook and Library Division, and the Georgia Library Association. The cataloging service was organized under the guidance of an Association committee whose members represented large and small school and public libraries and the Emory University Library School which helped plan the format of the cards and the method of distribution.

The service has been confined to books purchased through state channels, and State Cataloging Service is attempting to meet the demands for cards for uncataloged books already in libraries. During 1946-47 the cataloging service, staffed by two professional librarians and three clerks, was distributing an average of 5,000 sets of cards per month to 181 school libraries and 66 public libraries, including seven regional libraries.

29. Foltz, Florence P. "Cooperation Between the Public Libraries and the School Libraries in Denver, Colorado," *Illinois Libraries* 30: 166-68 (April 1948).

Pupils from schools are taken by their teachers on regular trips to the Denver Public Library where they are given a guided tour by the librarian. Students are encouraged to come to the public library for help with their school work. Statistics show that after these tours more students use, and continue to use, the public library. Librarians from the children's department of the public library in turn visit the schools giving book talks, book reviews, and displaying materials. In the few sections of the community where schools do not have good libraries, the public library has placed collections of books which are changed from time to time. In any school, classes may borrow special collections from the School Division of the Main Public Library for a period of 6-12 weeks. The public library also sends out a general collection of books to the school libraries from time to time. These books may be checked out by both pupils and adults in the community.

1949

30. Armstrong, Charles M.; McDiarmid, E. W.; Schenk, Gretchen K.; Van Deusen, Neil C.; Vedder, Agnes B. *Development of Library Services in New York State*. (New York [State] Univ. Bulletin no.1376) Albany: Univ. of the State of New York, 1949. 96p.

The authors are concerned with the establishment of regional service centers in New York State to serve public libraries. However they propose that these centers maintain union catalogs listing the holdings of public, school, and research libraries within the region. The union catalog would allow the Regional Service Center to determine what books were not in the region and needed to be purchased. Participation would be voluntary.

31. Henderson, John D. "The Regional Branch," in Carleton B. Joeckel, ed., *Reaching Readers; Techniques of Extending Library Service,* p.47-58. Berkeley: Univ. of California Pr., 1949.

Henderson writes of the use of schools to house branches of the Los Angeles County Public Library in the Antelope Valley area. The use of schools is dictated by financial pressures and is often unsatisfactory because of inadequate size and location of quarters assigned to the library.

32. Hill, Andrew P. "The Branch Library in the Public Schools," in Carleton B. Joeckel, ed., *Reaching Readers; Techniques of Extending Library Service,* p.59-66. Berkeley: Univ. of California Pr., 1949.

Hill describes the experience of Stockton (Calif.) in locating public library branches in the schools. New school buildings are planned to accommodate both school libraries and public library branches. The author argues that such an arrangement is workable and that economies in construction and maintenance costs can be realized while providing service to both school children and the neighborhood.

33. Zimmerman, Carma R. "Cooperation Among Independent and Affiliated Libraries," in Carleton B. Joeckel, ed., *Reaching Readers; Techniques of Extending Library Service,* p.88-104. Berkeley: Univ. of California Pr., 1949.

Several different examples of cooperation are described, including: (1) the Denver Public Library which cooperates with the Colorado Scientific Society and the licensed engineers of the state in the organization and extension of the library's technology department, by using surplus funds from the engineers' license fees for the purchase of technical and scientific books and periodicals; (2) the cooperation between Detroit Public Library and the Industrial Research Service which results in providing better reference service to industries and businesses in the Detroit area who underwrite the costs of the project; and (3) the Northwest Bibliographic Center (Seattle), an example of purposeful cooperation between all types of libraries in the region, whose most important function is the coordination of book resources in the region through the center's Subject Specialization Program.

34. *The Year's Work in Librarianship,* 1939-50, v.12-17. London: The Library Association, 1949-54.

Each of these volumes (except v.15; v.16 covers the years 1948 and 1949) contains a chapter entitled "Library Cooperation" which is devoted to a review of the literature and a discussion of developments in library cooperation. The emphasis is on activities in Great Britain, the British Commonwealth, and the United States, with briefer sections on international programs and other individual countries. Many of the items cited are included in the present bibliography, but the series is helpful for an overall perspective of the period and for its description of cooperative developments in England's regional systems.

35. Sampley, Arthur M. "Five Years of Library Cooperation in the North Texas Region," *College and Research Libraries* 10: 24-26 (Jan. 1949).

As a result of Dr. A. F. Kuhlman's recommendations *(see* item no.7) concerning cooperation between North Texas State Teachers College, Southern Methodist University, Texas Christian University, Texas State College for Women, Southwestern Baptist Theological Seminary, and the public libraries of Dallas and Fort Worth, some progress has been made. *The North Texas Regional Union List of Serials* has been completed and published in mimeographed form. One revision has already been made. Each cooperating library sent cards of their serial holdings to North Texas State Teachers College where the master card catalog was set up.

36. Allen, Francis W. "Cooperation in Boston," *Special Libraries* 40: 61-63 (Feb. 1949).

Allen describes the formation of an informal association of religious libraries in the greater Boston area. There are 22 member libraries, including eleven seminaries or colleges, six denominational headquarters, two independent interdenominational collections, two large active parish libraries, and one mission archives. Meetings have produced a number of concrete results. A satisfactory system of duplicate exchanges was worked out. Members of the group give each other free interlibrary loans and telephone reference service. A beginning has been made in the limitation of fields of purchase of the less popular and more expensive titles. The American Board Library and the Congregational Library are housed in the same building and share bibliographical tools and review periodicals; the General Theological Library and the Congregational Library cooperate in acquisition. General Theological is making itself responsible for all new material in general liturgics, while Congregational buys all significant publications in church architecture and in hymnology.

37. Wood, Susanna B. "A Plan for School Cooperation," *Library Occurrent* 16: 145-46 (March 1949).

The New Castle-Henry County (Ind.) Public Library provides bookmobile service to the New Castle public schools and maintains permanent collections in some elementary schools which enables them to serve as branch libraries. Book funds are pooled and salaries shared for trained personnel.

38. Myers, Walter E. "Cooperation Does Work," *Illinois Libraries* 31: 205-7 (May 1949).

Illinois State Library and the Institute of Labor and Industrial Relations of the University of Illinois are cooperating to give greater help to labor and industry of the state. The State Library sends library materials to any class, institute conference, workshop, or other meeting under the Institute's guidance. They offer a field visitor, special reading lists and local helps. The Institute Library affords technical service to the staff, answers research questions (though it does not lend books off campus), and provides extension courses and forum programs.

39. Stavely, Ronald. "An Inquiry into Cooperation," *Journal of Documentation* 5: 69-97 (Sept. 1949).

The Easter vacation course held at the School of Librarianship and Archives, University College, London, was a practical study of practices and problems of library cooperation in England. Public, national, university, government departments, learned society, and other special libraries were treated. The pros and cons of various forms of cooperation for each type of library were discussed.

The general attitude conveyed by the article was that cooperation had to greatly extend the availability of requested materials to warrant the extra time and staff necessary to support it.

40. Uridge, Margaret D. "Progress in Cooperation," *California Librarian* 11: 19-20, 35 (Sept. 1949).

The East Bay Librarians Council (San Francisco) surveyed the need for a regional warehouse to store little-used library materials. A committee was formed to organize a regional warehouse cooperative which would include all types of libraries—public, college, university, special—that would be interested in such a project.

Another cooperative project described in the San Francisco Bay area is the publication and distribution to research libraries of a list of library resources available in the region.

41. Pottinger, M. C. "The Farmington Plan: An American Experiment in Cooperation," *Library Association Record* 51: 306-10 (Oct. 1949).

After World War II, American librarians were concerned that many foreign books were not acquired for American libraries and also that a great deal of duplication existed in U.S. libraries. The success of the Library of Congress Mission for Cooperative Acquisition aided in starting the Farmington Plan for systematic cooperative book purchase. Under the plan there was a division of knowledge into 750 subject headings, and 54 libraries (both public and university) divided the subject areas primarily according to existing strengths. At first the plan was restricted to the book output of Sweden, Switzerland, and France; it was felt that the English output was handled sufficiently well. The plan began in January 1948 and at first the New York Public Library acted as the central office.

In 1949 Belgium, Norway, Denmark, Italy, Mexico, and the Netherlands were added to the plan. Each library that received a book under the plan notified the Library of Congress and a record of the book was put into the Union Catalog. Juvenile literature, precollege textbooks, translations from other modern languages, reprints, music scores, books in special format and those costing more than $25, sheet maps, periodicals, newspapers, numbered series issued by academic institutions or societies, theses, and government documents were not included in the plan. The first criticism of the Farmington Plan was that librarians were not choosing their own material; they were buying books which they might not acquire by their own selection.

42. "The Co-operative Provision of Books, Periodicals and Related Materials," *Library Association Record* 51: 383-87 (Dec. 1949).

This article presents a general discussion and plan for cooperative provision of materials in Great Britain with attention to objectives, types of users, completeness and duplication, concentration and separation, and types of coverage. In the plan the national and special libraries would act as research and bibliographical centers for all specialized information. A second line of libraries of all kinds would provide regional distribution, while major Regional Reference Libraries would furnish general reference and specialized materials for their regions. The general public's access to materials would be through lending libraries which, for the most part, are public libraries.

1950

43. Sewell, P. H. *The Regional Library Systems* (Library Association Pamphlet, no.2). London: Library Assn., 1950.

Sewell presents a description of the eight regional systems in England and Wales, the Regional Library Bureau of Scotland, the London Union Catalog, and the National Committee on Regional Library Co-operation. Brief histories are given together with a description of the services provided by each of the regional bureaus and their means of support. Union catalogs and interlibrary lending are the principal services provided.

44. Lamb, J. P. "The Interchange of Technical Publications in Sheffield," *Aslib Proceedings* 2: 41-48 (Feb. 1950).

The creation of the Interchange of Technical Publications in Sheffield (England) in 1933 is fully discussed as an early example of cooperation between public libraries and the libraries of manufacturers. In 1933, 100 loans or exchanges of materials took place; by 1948, the number of loans and exchanges among an expanded membership had reached 1,380. Innovations in the system since World War II are discussed.

45. Scurfield, Jannetta G. "Interlibrary Co-Operation: The Regional Library Bureau," *Aslib Proceedings* 2: 77-80 (May 1950).

Scurfield explains Great Britain's interlibrary lending system in which libraries—public, university, and special—pool their book stocks in a nationwide system of mutual cooperation. Over 700 libraries participate. England is divided into ten regions, nine of which have a Regional Library Bureau, which acts in a clearinghouse capacity for the applications for the books which are wanted by the libraries in its own and other areas. The Regional Bureaus maintain union catalogs which record the nonfiction books available; a master union catalog is maintained by the National Central Library in London.

Scurfield illustrates the workings of the system, lists some of the restrictions on materials which can be borrowed, and discusses some of the problems which the plan solves.

46. Gelfand, Morris A. "Library Cooperation in Metropolitan New York: Report of Work in Progress," *College and Research Libraries* 11: 245-49 (July 1950).

The author reports on the work of committees formed by 26 New York librarians representing different types of libraries to investigate possibilities for library cooperation in the area. The committees are discussing what areas of cooperation should be investigated.

47. Lewis, Helen B. "Cleveland Public Library Runs School Libraries," *Library Journal* 75: 1102-5 (July 1950).

A concrete example of interlibrary cooperation involving the Cleveland Public Library and the Board of Education is given by the author. The Cleveland Board of Education furnishes the physical plant and maintenance of the school libraries, provides a book budget, pays the salaries of some staff members, and pays for the cataloging and binding of books. The Public Library appoints all personnel and pays the salaries for the supervisory services and selects the books. During the summer months, the School Department staff may be assigned to work at the Main Library or other branches. Although the libraries in schools are branches of the Public Library, they remain separate except for four elementary school libraries located in the outlying areas which give limited service to the community.

48. Metcalf, Keyes D. "Proposal for a Northeastern Regional Library," *College and Research Libraries* 11: 238-44 (July 1950).

Metcalf proposes the formation of a Northeastern Regional Library to include Harvard, Yale, Columbia, New York Public Library, Princeton, Pennsylvania, Boston Public Library, and the Massachusetts State Library as initial members. The new library will help take care of less used, bulky collections and eliminate unnecessary duplication.

The author also proposes that smaller libraries be allowed to join the regional library if they so desire. Metcalf suggests that, to begin with, the Regional Library might take over books from member libraries in eight different categories with six others to be considered later. All material in these categories would be sent to the regional library for permanent deposit so duplicates could be weeded.

Metcalf does not discuss cooperative buying and cataloging for fear of making the initial plan too complicated. A possible exception would be Farmington Plan books which could be sent directly to the regional library where they would be cataloged at the expense of the regional library.

49. White, Carl M. "A New Mechanism in the Organization of Library Service in the Northeast," *College and Research Libraries* 11: 228-37 (July 1950).

White reports on the views of three New York City committees formed to study the possibility of a regional library. The committees envisaged a central cooperative library, among whose activities would be the acquisition and housing of publications, the distribution of catalog cards, and the photographic reproduction of library materials—emphatically this was not to be just a "dead" storage library. Starting at this point, White proposes a positive acquisitions program along the following lines:

- The Northeastern Regional Library is to be responsible for the full coverage of:
  - publications of importance for research which are originally intended for a limited public
  - important publications for research in less-used languages
  - important research publications which, because of obsolescence, serve only a limited audience
- The Northeastern Regional Library should freely delegate responsibility for limited audience material to other libraries, but it would not be able to impose such commitments
- The Northeastern Regional Library would accept custody for little-used materials from other libraries.

50. "Just What Is a Regional Cooperative Library?" *Library Journal* 75: 1365, 1369-72 (1 Sept. 1950).

The proposals of the Committee on the Division of Subject Fields of a group known as "Cooperation among Libraries of Metropolitan New York" are discussed. The Committee includes university, public, and special librarians and is concerned with plans for a Regional Cooperative Library for the New York area. The Regional Cooperative Library would offer inexpensive storage for member libraries and actively collect to further develop the collections put in its care. It would also collect in all fields not adequately covered by member libraries. The main aim of the regional library would be the reduction of duplication by discarding, selling, or exchanging of materials.

51. Turgason, Anna J. "School-Public Library Systems," *Clearing House* 25: 226-29 (Dec. 1950).

The four junior high school libraries in Racine (Wis.) operate as branches of the public library. Two are open to the public and two serve elementary school children. This article points out some of the advantages of this arrangement in supplying materials and describes the general operation of the junior high school libraries.

1951

52. Campion, Eleanor Este. "The Philadelphia Bibliographical Center and Union Library Catalog," *Bulletin of the Special Libraries Council of Philadelphia and Vicinity* 17, no.2: 9-13 (Jan. 1951).

This covers the development of the Union Catalog of Philadelphia and its subsequent change to a bibliographic center. The basic file of three and a half million cards represented the holdings of 168 cooperating college, university, public, historical, and special libraries. In 15 years the file increased by one million cards and the number of cooperating libraries by twelve college and special libraries. Financial support is presently derived from cooperating libraries, industrial firms, and private donations. The University of Pennsylvania houses the center in its Fine Arts Buildings. Data on use of the center are included.

53. Carter, Harriet I. "The Indiana Plan for Extension Services," *Library Occurrent* 16: 361-68 (Dec. 1950). (Partially reprinted as the "Federation Idea," *Public Libraries* 5: 49 [April 1951]).

Indiana's new plan for library extension services provides that, in so far as possible, the state extension service will work toward cooperation and coordination of all types of libraries in the region. It was also proposed that a specialist field worker work with the school library adviser in coordinating public libraries and school libraries.

54. McAnally, Arthur M. "Recent Developments in Cooperation," *College and Research Libraries* 12: 123-32 (April 1951).

Library cooperation is discussed under a number of different headings such as interlibrary loans, photographic reproduction, duplicate exchanges, local and regional cooperation, and cooperation on a national level. Special projects that are discussed include the Farmington Plan, United States Book Exchange, the Midwest Inter-Library Center, the Regional Council for Education in the South, the Denver Bibliographical Center, the Cooperative Acquisitions Project, the Documents Expediting Project, and the Cooperative Committee on Library Buildings. This is a comprehensive and important article on library cooperation.

55. Orvig, Mary. "Stockholm Cooperative Program," *Wilson Library Bulletin* 25: 620-21 (April 1951).

Twenty-one of Stockholm's (Sweden) 49 public library branches are housed in school buildings and have cooperative programs with the schools. Thirty-two other public schools have coordinated their activities with the City Library.

Branches situated in public schools serve as school libraries during the day and are staffed by the schools. In the evenings the branches serve as children's departments of the City Library which provides the staff.

The City Library assumes responsibility for reorganization of the school libraries, for technical processes, and for book selection in consultation with teacher-librarians.

56. "Public Library Bookmobile Service to Schools," *ALA Bulletin* 45: 131-32 (April 1951).

This report by the Committee of the State School Library Supervisors and the ALA Library Extension Division attempts to set down basic principles, requirements, and advantages of a public library bookmobile service to schools to supplement the library materials supplied by the school itself. No specific examples are mentioned.

57. Willett, Mary A. "It Works in Lakewood," *Library Journal* 76: 833-34, 836 (15 May 1951).

In Lakewood (Ind.) the school libraries are administered by a cooperative arrangement between the Public Library and the Board of Education in which the Board of Education assumes responsibility for all equipment and for materials closely associated with classroom instruction. The public library buys materials for recreational and general reading and provides ordering and cataloging for school library materials. Reference and interlibrary loan service are facilitated by trunk line connections between the public libraries and the schools.

58. "Library Co-Operation, A Symposium," in The Library Association, *Proceedings, Papers and Summaries of Discussions at the Edinburgh Conference, 5th to 8th June 1951,* p.49-62. London: The Association, 1951.

There were three papers read at this symposium: (1) "Special Libraries" by Wilfred Pearson; (2) "Reference Libraries" by Edward Hargreaves; (3) "Co-operation between Libraries Specializing in the Social Sciences" by A. J. Walford and Barbara Kyle. The article on special libraries points out the great amount of interlending of books and periodicals and discusses the problem of tracing sources of holdings. Pearson urges that union lists of periodical holdings be produced. The Hargreaves article looks forward to greater cooperation between reference and special libraries. The purpose of the Walford and Kyle paper is "to indicate what is being done, particularly in London, by way of cooperative effort between libraries specializing in the social sciences, to note one or two international trends, and finally to suggest what lines might profitably be followed in order to make the literature of the social sciences more available."

59. Krarup, Agnes. "Cooperation in Pittsburgh," *National Elementary Principal* 31: 217-22 (Sept. 1951).

Cooperation between public and elementary school libraries in Pittsburgh in the early 1950s is described fully. Public libraries aid in book processing and cooperate in book selection.

60. Bauer, Harry. "Interpreting the PNBC in Terms of Human Relations," *Pacific Northwest Library Association Quarterly* 16: 25-27 (Oct. 1951).

Bauer describes the Pacific Northwest Bibliographic Center which gives service to all types of libraries in the region. The center has no books but provides the key to the holdings of 39 major libraries in the region in addition to those of the Library of Congress and the John Crerar Library. The objectives of the center are: to make all the books of the region available to all libraries through interlibrary loans, to build and strengthen regional library holdings through pooling collections by means of the Bibliographic Center, and to prevent loss of unique items through a regional discarding program.

The Pacific Northwest Bibliographic Center is very successful. Cooperation is entirely voluntary.

61. Chapman, Eulalia D. "Denver Bibliographical Center," *Medical Library Association Bulletin* 39: 284-89 (Oct. 1951).

Chapman discusses the functions and activities of the Denver Bibliographical Center located at Denver Public Library. Public libraries, college and research libraries, and special libraries are members. The membership fee for public libraries is based on population served and for college libraries on student enrollment; additional service charges are based on the use of the center by each participating library.

A reference collection of more than 10,000 volumes is held by the center whose main objectives are:

- To assemble and maintain bibliographical collections, resources, aids, and materials essential for planning research and scholarly investigation
- To maintain a union catalog of member libraries and other libraries
- To develop a center and bureau of information for interlibrary loans between member libraries in the region
- To maintain a close relationship with the Library of Congress and its Union Catalog
- To further cooperation and coordination of resources and services among the libraries of the Rocky Mountain Region.

62. Wiese, Bernice, et al. "We Work Together," *Library Journal* 76: 2052-55 (15 Dec. 1951).

Cooperation between school and public libraries in Baltimore is directed by a Joint Administrative Committee representing both types of libraries. Some of the cooperative activities have been the publication of "The High School Librarians Choose," an annual reading list for school children; discussions about what books each library will buy to get the best coverage, particularly in the area of expensive reference works; and the lending of public library books to teachers in public and parochial schools for classroom work. In addition public librarians give book talks to school classes and classes visit the local public library.

All divisions of the public library assist the Department of Education in its teaching program. Teachers receive bibliographies and materials for lesson planning. Adult education classes of the public schools often meet in branch library auditoriums and make use of the public library's collections.

1952

63. Armstrong, Charles M. "The First Three Years of the Regional Plan for Library Development in Lewis, Jefferson and St. Lawrence Counties." [Albany]: Univ. of the State of New York, State Education Dept., Div. of Research, 1952. 98*l*. Mimeographed.

Armstrong deals with cooperation between public libraries, but some instances of interlibrary cooperation between other types of libraries are mentioned. The Regional Center of the district offers service for the general public in the school libraries in Parishville, Winthrop-St. Lawrence, and West Leydon, but few adults make use of this service. In Russell the public library and school library are in the same room in the school building. The librarian is an employee of the school and responsible to the school principal as well as to the public library board. Again only a few adults avail themselves of this service.

In Port Leydon the public library is located in a school building but in a room of its own. Adults are not made welcome to use the school library's reference volumes, and the community is too small to afford two separate sets of reference materials.

64. Vollans, Robert F. *Library Cooperation in Great Britain, Report of a Survey of the National Central Library and the Regional Library Bureaux.* London: The National Central Library, 1952. 139p.

This survey of library cooperation, done at the request of the Joint Working Party of the Executive Committee of the National Central Library and the National Committee on Regional Library Co-operation, presents a brief history of the development of the National Central Library and Great Britain's system of regional library bureaus. Aspects pertaining to cooperation are concerned chiefly with interlibrary loans and the part which the regional bureaus, the National Central Library, public, university, and special libraries play in the scheme. Union catalogs and subject specialization are also considered.

65. Mahoney, R. E. "Federated Libraries," *Library Journal* 77: 15-20 (1 Jan. 1952).

Library cooperation in twelve metropolitan areas aimed at providing better service in suburban areas is described. The Buffalo (N.Y.) and the San Francisco Bay area federations are described in detail.

66. Clark, Edward. "School Libraries by Contract," *Library Journal* 77: 108-9 (15 Jan. 1952).

The Springfield (Ohio) Board of Education has contracted since 1920 with the Warder Public Library of Clark County for the provision of school library materials. The board of education provides funds for the purchase of materials, and for reimbursement of staff time spent on processing school materials. The board of education is also responsible for providing quarters and equipment and transportation of materials between the schools and the public libraries. The public library agrees to select, order, and process materials and to provide binding arrangements. A questionnaire survey has indicated satisfaction with the plan.

67. Brown, Keith G. "The Need for Co-ordinating Between Public and University Libraries and Special Libraries of Corporations," *Texas Library Journal* 28: 17-22 (March 1952).

This article discusses how public libraries can give service to the growing number of special libraries. It suggests that a beginning could be made if public libraries would survey their resources of materials and personnel, and, if possible, prepare definite codes for serving industry. Such codes should cover loan procedures of books normally lent to the public, the loan of books not normally circulated, the loan of magazines, and telephone service.

68. Sherwood, Janice W. and Campion, Eleanor E. "Union Library Catalogue: Services, 1950. Quo Vadis?" *College and Research Libraries* 13: 101-6, 110 (April 1952).

This article reports on an inquiry into the effectiveness of regional union catalogs. Questionnaires were sent to the Union Catalog Division of the Library of Congress, the Union Library Catalog of the Philadelphia Metropolitan Area, the Pacific Northwest Bibliographical Center, the Bibliographical Center for Research at Denver, and the Union Catalog at the Western Reserve University Library in Cleveland. Questions asked related to the type of clientele served, the number of questions answered, bibliographical tools and services, special services, regional cooperation, national cooperation, special files, publications, organization and financial support, and an estimate of services rendered.

The survey reports that services are particularly valuable for the immediate areas served by the centers and that the expenditures bring a worthwhile return.

69. Dennis, Willard. "School and Regional Libraries Combine," *School and Community* 38: 238-41 (May 1952).

The writer describes the gains in economy, efficiency of service, and physical facilities effected by placement of the Dallas County Headquarters collection of the Southwest Regional Library on a school campus.

70. "How Louisiana Compiled a Union Free Film Catalog," *Library Journal* 77: 1066 (15 June 1952).

The Louisiana State Library, with the help of a Carnegie grant, completed a union catalog of all films available for free statewide circulation. The catalog lists all 16mm films from state, federal, private, and commercial agencies. There are 855 film titles listed as available from 66 film lending agencies. The original intention was to house the card catalog in the Louisiana State Library, but since funds were available, the catalog was printed. The catalog will be distributed on request to libraries, statewide organizations, and other agencies which use films.

71. "Vermont's Union Catalog," *Bulletin of the Free Public Library Commission and of the State Library* [Vermont] 48: 18-23 (Sept. 1952).

The article describes Vermont's Union Catalog of adult nonfiction of approximately half a million cards located in the office of the Free Library Commission in Montpelier. College, university, public, and special libraries contribute cards on a voluntary basis in an attempt to improve interlibrary loan service and to provide possibilities for future cooperation in acquisition and discarding.

72. "What About A Storage Library?" *California Librarian* 14: 33 (Sept. 1952).

Two hundred eighty-three libraries in northern California were queried by the Committee on Regional Cooperation, California Library Association, on the feasibility of a central storage library. Most of the 85 respondents reported little need for such a center, but felt that a cooperative acquisitions program should be part of any such center established.

73. "Films are Available Through Illinois State Library," *Illinois Libraries* 34:381-82 (Nov. 1952).

Over 9,000 prints covering 3,000 separate titles are now offered to Illinois residents free through an agreement between the Illinois State Library and the Visual Aids Service of the University of Illinois. The only cost to the borrower is postage to return the film to the University.

The service is offered to all local communities and is used primarily by the public libraries.

1953

74. Brahm, Walter. "Legal Status of Public Libraries," *Library Trends* 1: 471-81 (April 1953).

The author tells of New Hampshire State Library's use of bookmobiles to give supplementary aid to public and school libraries which are not open daily in an attempt to cover all sections of the state.

75. Collison, R. L. W. "Aspects of Co-operation in University and Special Libraries in the United States of America," in *Proceedings, Papers and Summaries of Discussions at the Llandudno Conference, 28th April to 1st May 1953*, p.43-49. London: The Library Assn., 1953.

Among the general areas of cooperation between academic and special libraries noted are:

- The exchange of catalog cards: John Crerar Library, Morgan Library, Folger Shakespeare Library, William Andrews Clark Memorial Library, and Princeton University Library have distributed printed cards of acquisitions to interested libraries

- Cooperative planning of book purchases: the John Crerar Library, Chicago Public Library, and Newberry Library have a long-standing agreement on which subject fields each will cover; the Linda Hall Library works very closely with the Kansas City (Mo.) Public Library and the University of Kansas School of Medicine. A set of the main entry cards of Linda Hall Library are deposited in the Science and Technology Division of Kansas City Public Library

- Provision of storage and deposit facilities: several special libraries contribute to Midwest Inter-Library Center (MILC, now Center for Research Libraries) in Chicago. The Philadelphia Bibliographical Center and Union Library Catalog (founded in 1935) serves all types of libraries in Pennsylvania and Delaware. In addition, a few special libraries participate in the Rocky Mountain Regional Bibliographical Center for Research in Denver.

76. McColvin, Lionel R. "English Public Libraries," *Library Trends* 1: 522-30 (April 1953).

McColvin writes of Britain's nationwide system of regional bureaus. The bureaus include all public and a great many special nonpublic libraries. The National Central Library serves as the coordinating unit.

77. Ardern, L. L. "Information, Industry and Integration," *Library Association Record* 55: 158-60 (May 1953).

The author describes the operation of the North-Western Regional Library Bureau (England) for requests of an advanced scientific or technical nature. Most requests for such materials are handled by two university libraries, the Manchester College of Technology Library, and a half-dozen industrial libraries. This article and the commentary by S. P. L. Filon suggest that special libraries are not getting the service they require from the regional systems as they are currently operating. He proposes the creation of separate "Special Library Bureaux" which could cooperate closely with existing "Regional Bureaux."

78. Fuller, Helen and Josselyn, Clara, "Public and School Libraries Cooperate," *Wilson Library Bulletin* 27: 716-17 (May 1953).

In Long Beach (Calif.) the public library sends a children's librarian to visit school classes twice a year. Schools and the public library also cooperate in the selection of materials for beginning readers and in the sponsorship of a summer reading program for beginning grades.

79. Dunn, Oliver. "Bibliographical Cooperation in California: A Survey of Highlights," *California Librarian* 14: 246-47 (June 1953).

This is an inventory of cooperative bibliographic projects completed or underway in California. Among the projects is a regional catalog of phonograph records, initiated by the northern chapter of the Music Library Association and housed in the San Francisco State College Library. Four projects are concerned with materials in southern California libraries: (1) a union catalog of bibliographies; (2) a union list of botanical books and serials; (3) a union list of local documents; and (4) materials on the Pacific area which consist of a series of union lists published by Claremont College from 1939-1944.

Other projects include a union list of periodicals in the San Francisco Bay Region, a 1947 map of book resources in the same area, and a survey of special resources in California libraries.

80. Brown, J. W. "Film Center Services to Libraries," *Washington State Library—Library News Bulletin* 20: 149 (Sept.-Oct. 1953).

Brown reports the progress made since 1951 by the University of Washington Film Center in distributing 16mm sound films on a month-long basis to several public libraries in the state. "Public Film Library Statistics," a report issued 22 May 1953 by the American Library Association showed that Washington public libraries "exceeded every other circuit in the nation in average circulation per print (9.8 per print per month)."

The article also gives the specific provisions and costs for renting films from the University of Washington Film Center. School libraries are not included in this plan.

81. Morsch, Lucile M. "Cooperation and Centralization," *Library Trends* 2: 342-55 (Oct. 1953).

A discussion of the possibilities and advantages of centralized cataloging together with a number of successful examples is presented.

In Norway, school and rural public libraries order their books through the Folkeboksamlingenes Ekspedisjon which also catalogs all the books. The Deichmanske Bibliothek in Oslo prints its catalog cards and makes them available, by subscription, to other libraries.

In Russia the State Publishing House for Culture and Education, the Leningrad Public Library, and the All-Union Book Chamber print catalog cards and make them available to other libraries. The cards are, however, used primarily for bibliographic purposes other than for catalogs.

In Brazil, a centralized cataloging agency, the Servicio de Intercambio de Catalogacao (SIC), furnishes each cooperating library 15 copies of its own cards. The copy is edited and printed by the Imprensa National. The system closely resembles that of the Library of Congress.

The National Diet Library in Japan makes cards available for the books it catalogs to about 50 libraries.

In the United States, Georgia's State Cataloging Service is operated for public school libraries by the State Department of Education. Libraries receive "dictionary sets" of mimeographed cards for all books purchased from state funds for school and public libraries.

82. Orr, Marion. "A Public Library Cooperates with the Schools," *Idaho Librarian* 5: 17-19 (Oct. 1953).

Taken from the 1952-1953 annual report of the Idaho Falls Public Library, the article describes public library-school cooperation as it existed at that time.

83. Sams, Mrs. Arch. "Regional Library Service in Clark and Skamania Counties," *Pacific Northwest Library Association Quarterly* 18: 53-54 (Oct. 1953).

Mrs. Sams mentions a contract between two schools in Skamania County with Fort Vancouver Regional Library for bookmobile service.

84. Ball, Alice D. "Exchange Supermarket," *Library Journal* 78: 2057-61 (1 Dec. 1953).

The United States Book Exchange, Inc. (USBE) is a private, nonprofit (but self-supporting) organization which performs exchange operations for 500 large and small, foreign and American member libraries of all types. These libraries contribute any number of publications and in return can receive any quantity. Altogether one-half million publications are received at USBE every year.

The member libraries send requests for wanted items directly to USBE. If the materials are not in stock the request is held until the order can be filled. This works especially well with periodicals. They can be ordered directly, even before appearing on an exchange list. Because of the large numbers of periodicals in stock and daily receipts, this service offers one of the surest, quickest, as well as cheapest ways for libraries to receive back issues.

85. "News Notes from the States, Operation Cooperation." *Public Libraries* 7, no.4: 12-15, 18 (Dec. 1953).

Public Libraries asked state agencies to send them instances of interlibrary cooperation in their states. This article lists briefly some of the examples. Instances cited range from cooperation in acquisitions, union catalogs, and lists of films and other specialized materials to contracts for service and other less formal arrangements.

86. "School-Public Library Service," *Library Occurrent* 17: 356 (Dec. 1953).

This article reports on a questionnaire survey of school and public library relationships in Indiana. The findings indicate that few libraries have a definite policy on duplication of services and materials or any plan for cooperative selection. Furnishing classroom collections and instruction in the use of the public library appear to be the services most commonly provided by the public library.

A series of institutes sponsored by the State Department of Public Instruction and the State Library on the functions of school and public libraries and ways the two may cooperate have also been held. Discussion sessions hopefully were to lead to recommendations to the Indiana State Library Association.

1954

87. Schenk, Gretchen K. *County and Regional Library Development.* Chicago: American Library Assn., 1954. 263p.

New York's regional service center, established in Watertown in 1948, offers books, materials, and advisory services to any existing library in the three-county region. The Erie County Public Library, organized in 1948, is essentially a federation of the Buffalo Public Library, the Grosvenor Reference Library, and 23 established libraries outside the city of Buffalo. Both services are reported as working well.

88. Carter, Harriet I. "An Experiment in Cooperation," *Library Occurrent* 18: 19-21 (Jan. 1954).

The author reports on a series of 16 institutes held throughout Indiana on cooperation between school and public libraries.

89. Esterquest, Ralph T. "Midwest Inter-Library Center: Acquisition Policy and Program, 1950-53," *College and Research Libraries* 15: 47-49, 89 (Jan. 1954).

Esterquest provides a description of the acquisitions program of the Midwest Inter-Library Center (now Center for Research Libraries). This is based on a concept of sharing in the use of those library items which the individual member libraries do not wish to acquire because the cost of individual ownership is too high. The center is trying to develop a service operation, not a book collection as such. The center's "collection" is only an adjunct to the basic research collections of the member libraries. The center buys a book if (1) it is not owned by or is not easily available in one of the participating libraries; (2) it is little used; and (3) it has value in terms of the research purposes of the region.

The center avoids duplicating fields of specialization that exist in the region or elsewhere in the country. The selection of materials for the center is in the hands of the participating librarians. In 1953 it was decided that the center should inaugurate a program for "transferring subscriptions." Each library will review its periodical subscription list for the purpose of dropping rarely consulted items which the center would agree to acquire. A typical member library, it was felt, could trim its list by 10-20 percent without impairing its service in any serious way. Most members of MILC are university libraries, but reference libraries such as John Crerar can also be members.

90. Hodgson, James G. *Regional Library Cooperation in the Rocky Mountain Region and the Northern Great Plains, 1935-1953: A Bibliography.* (Bulletin no.10) Denver: Bibliographical Center for Research—Rocky Mountain Region, Feb. 1954.

This bibliography covers "publications of and about the Bibliographical Center for Research—Rocky Mountain Region, the Colorado College and Head Librarians Conference, the Mountain-Plains Library Association, and the Northern Great Plains Library Planning Council." It includes annual reports, minutes of meetings, publications describing the work of those organizations, and other related materials.

91. Blodgett, Philip R. "Interlibrary Loan, A New Approach," *Pacific Northwest Library Association Quarterly* 18: 125-29 (April 1954).

In 1952 the president of the Washington Library Association appointed a committee to study the question of interlibrary loan service in the state of Washington. The system in effect at that time required that Washington libraries submit interlibrary loan requests first to the Washington State Library. Unfilled requests were sent to the Pacific Northwest Bibliographic Center. The committee suggested a twelve-point plan to improve the service. The main feature of the plan is that interlibrary loan requests be sent first to the Seattle Public Library instead of the State Library, since it was anticipated that the public library would be able to fill a greater number of requests. The State Library was to support a special interlibrary loan staff at Seattle Public Library.

92. Williams, Edwin E. "Exchanges: National and International," *Library Trends* 2: 562-72 (April 1954).

Williams describes the United States Book Exchange (USBE) founded in 1948. The organization accepts for exchange credit unsorted and unlisted lots of "monographs in science and technology published during the last ten years, or those published in the humanities, the arts or history during the last 15 years as well as organized classics of older date. There is no date limit on periodicals, which are acceptable in the same fields, both scattered issues and long runs." Lists arranged by language or country are distributed regularly, and requests for any publication that the exchange might have or may later acquire may be submitted on forms that sell for 10¢. A library receiving material from the exchange pays for postage and handling fees ranging from 10¢ to $1.

93. Bates, Mary. "Regional Libraries," *Tennessee Librarian* 6: 149-50 (June 1954).

The regional libraries of Tennessee are planning to sponsor adult education in the use of library facilities. They feel that the University of Tennessee Extension Division might be able to help with an in-service training program and with an adult education program to train discussion leaders.

94. Warner, Gilmore. "Union Catalog of Films," *Pennsylvania Library Association Bulletin* 10: 3-4 (Summer 1954).

The Union Catalog of Films at Lock Haven State College (Lock Haven, Pa.) lists holdings of films of libraries which cooperate in the project and makes location information available to patrons on request. A similar program in Illinois makes films in the University of Illinois film library available to public libraries in the state.

95. Eaton, Andrew J. "The Place of College and University Libraries in the Development of Public Library Services in Missouri," *Missouri Library Association Quarterly* 15: 57-62 (Sept. 1954).

The guiding principle of the Missouri Libraries Planning Committee is that full cooperation between all types of libraries—school, college and university, private or special—must be accomplished to further the library development of the state as a whole.

The author suggests how academic libraries can contribute to library development in the state:

- By providing supplementary book, reference, and bibliographical services
- By making plans for the improved coverage and accessibility of specialized materials
- By providing training for public library staff members
- By supporting the work of the state library and the state library association.

96. Harshe, Florence E. "Small Libraries Progress Together in Watertown Region," *Minnesota Libraries* 18: 336-38 (Sept. 1954).

The article discusses cooperation between public libraries, but there is some mention of four central school libraries, serving as public libraries in the Watertown (Minn.) area.

97. Longworth, Ruth O. "Glacier County Library; An Example of Cooperation," *Wilson Library Bulletin* 29: 73-74 (Sept. 1954).

The author describes cooperation between the Glacier County Library in Cut Bank (Mont.) and two high school libraries—one in Cut Bank, the other in Browning. The county librarian supervises both high school libraries and does the purchasing and processing of books for both libraries. During the summer the county librarian trains student librarians who supervise the school libraries during the school year.

98. Metcalf, Keyes D. "The New England Deposit Library After Thirteen Years," *Harvard Library Bulletin* 8: 313-22 (Autumn 1954).

Metcalf discusses Harvard's participation in the New England Deposit Library. The main aim of the scheme, to provide inexpensive storage, has been fully achieved. The enterprise is more successful financially than anticipated. It has also been demonstrated that the inconvenience entailed in storing books at a distance from the main collection is minimal, since the materials accounted for less than 1 percent of total use.

The major problem has been the selection of materials for the storage library. Harvard has removed whole subject classes (agriculture, education textbooks, and the like), large and bulky sets, some newly acquired materials which were expected to have little use, and individual volumes which were little used.

99. Homeyer, B. C. "Zachary Taylor Library Gives Municipal, County, College Service," *Texas Library Journal* 30: 197-99 (Dec. 1954).

The Zachary Taylor Library (Brownsville, Tex.) is operated by both the City of Brownsville and Texas Southmost College. The library is directed by the college librarian who is responsible for the dual functions of serving both the college and the city. The library is housed in a wing of the city's Fort Brown Memorial Center which is a multipurpose civic facility. A floor plan of the library is included in the article.

1955

100. Esterquest, Ralph T. *Library Cooperation in the British Isles.* (ACRL Monograph, no.12) Chicago: Assn. of College and Research Libraries, American Library Assn., 1955. 24p.

In this survey, Esterquest discusses several examples of interlibrary cooperation in the British Isles. The National Central Library is the center of the regional system which covers the entire country. Public libraries and occasionally university libraries support the regional bureaus financially and contribute holdings information to their union catalogs and send to them their requests for interlibrary loans. The system enables any person within the British Isles to borrow any book wanted for a reasonably serious purpose, provided there is a copy somewhere in the regional system.

The Sheffield Inter-Change Scheme was inaugurated in 1933. There are 40 members, including the University of Sheffield, Sheffield Public Library, scientific societies, and libraries of industrial establishments. Member libraries lend freely to each other; a union list of scientific and technical periodicals has been compiled to help interlibrary loan work.

The Cooperative Industrial and Commercial Reference and Information Service plan (CICRIS) operates in the western outskirts of London. Centered in the Acton Public Library, it has the support of the public library authorities in the area as well as a growing number of industrial, research, and institutional establishments. The plan attempts to provide a clearinghouse for all local sources of information, with emphasis on commerce and industry.

The main effort in developing a national plan of library specialization is directed by the Working Party on the Cooperative Provision of Books, Periodicals, and Related Materials in Libraries, formed by the Library Association in 1949. The aim of the Working Party is to develop a national specialization plan to ensure that "everything useful shall be available somewhere and for the common benefit."

101. Hunt, K. G. *Subject Specialisation and Cooperative Book Purchase in the Libraries of Great Britain.* (Library Assn. Pamphlet, no.12) London: The Library Assn., 1955. 32p.

Hunt describes all cooperative book purchasing schemes known to be in existence in Great Britain and Northern Ireland at the end of April 1954. Several of the schemes involve a combination of public, university, and special libraries. One of these was developed under the aegis of the Joint Standing Committee on Library Cooperation and was aimed at the provision of seventeenth and eighteenth century background materials, i.e., materials used in certain types of research though not normally classified as source materials. By January 1954, 19 university, 10 special, and 24 public libraries were involved in the project.

Other cooperative schemes are organized on a regional basis and frequently involve university and public libraries. In the Northern Region there is a plan for a Joint Reserve Stock of Fiction in which the University of Durham participates with the public libraries. The East Midlands has a program for the provision of foreign language materials in which both university and public libraries take part. In Wales and Monmouthshire cooperative acquisition is practiced with a number of libraries having indicated the subject areas in which they wish to specialize. Most of these plans have been designed to facilitate interlibrary loans.

102. Lamb, J. P. "The Organization for the Interchange of Technical Publications in Sheffield and District," *Serial Slants* 6: 6-14 (Jan. 1955).

The Sheffield scheme for the interchange of technical publications between the Science and Commerce Library (a public library) and the libraries of industrial concerns and businesses in the area is fully explained.

103. Ashworth, Wilfred. "Special Libraries and Library Cooperation in South Wales and Monmouthshire," *Library Association Record* 58: 60-62 (Feb. 1955).

Although special libraries cannot cooperate directly in the subject specialization scheme adopted by the regional library bureaus in 1953, many special libraries notify the bureaus of expensive purchases which are not duplicated by the public libraries in the area. Also, a holdings list of scientific periodicals in Glamorgan and Monmouth has been published.

104. David, Charles W., and Hirsch, Rudolf. "Cooperation and Planning from the Regional Viewpoint," *Library Trends* 3: 356-75 (April 1955).

The need for cooperative acquisitions on a regional or local basis is discussed and some of the existing programs are described. The division of subject fields between the New York Public Library and Columbia University, agreed on in 1896, was no longer an effective guide to selection policy. More effective is Columbia's decision to rely on the New York Academy of Medicine. Columbia University, the American Museum of National History, and the New York Botanical Gardens have cooperative purchase arrangements in several biological fields.

Other cooperative agreements mentioned include Enoch Pratt Free Library's agreement with the Historical Society and the Peabody Institute for the collection of "Maryland materials"; it is described by the authors as moderately successful. Nashville libraries have cooperated in serials acquisition and, in Cleveland, specialization has been distributed among university, public, and several special libraries. Also described is the long-term plan followed by John Crerar, Newberry, and the Chicago Public Library.

Three regional schemes described are the Rocky Mountain and the Pacific Northwest Bibliographic Centers and the Midwest Inter-Library Center, now the Center for Research Libraries.

105. Wemmer, Frederick. "Coordinating Library Resources," *California Librarian* 16: 187-89 (April 1955).

Wemmer describes the work and activities of the Regional Resources Coordinating Committee of the California Library Association, which was organized to survey the research resources in California and to initiate and promote cooperative projects in making these resources known and available.

The major undertaking with which the committee has been associated is the volume, *California Local History, a Centennial Bibliography,* edited by Ethel Blumann and Mabel W. Thomas, and published by the Stanford University Press.

106. Selby, Mildred. "The Public Library and the Boise Elementary Schools," *Idaho Librarian* 7: 51-52 (July 1955).

A reading program was provided by the public library with the cooperation of elementary school teachers. The goal of the project was to get nonreaders to read. Children who read four books during the spring months were permitted to sign their names to a reading chart. The aim was to get full participation in all of the classes. Teachers were encouraged to hear reports on books read by the children. The success of the program has severely taxed the staff and resources of the public library.

107. Edmonds, May. "Miami Public Report on Cataloging Experiment for the Dade County Schools," *Journal of Cataloging and Classification* 11: 216-17 (Oct. 1955).

The lack of a centralized ordering and processing procedure for school library materials, combined with a sudden increase in the number of school operating units, in Dade County (Fla.), led to serious problems in handling new materials. To cope with the problems, an experimental project was initiated between the county school libraries and the Miami Public Library in which the public library ordered, cataloged, and classified a basic collection of 500 books for one of Dade County's new elementary schools. The school paid for the cost of the books plus a 70¢ service charge for each book handled.

No formal agreements for continuation of the program were reported.

1956

108. Wilson, Louis Round, and Tauber, Maurice F. "Cooperation and Specialization," in *The University Library; The Organization, Administration, and Functions of Academic* Libraries, p.449-80. 2d ed. New York: Columbia Univ. Pr., 1956.

The largest area of cooperation between university and other types of libraries is in interlibrary loan. Union catalogs can also involve university libraries with public or special libraries, e.g., the Union Library Catalog of the Philadelphia Metropolitan Area. Sometimes there are agreements for specialization in collecting such as the one between the University of Chicago, John Crerar, and Newberry Libraries. Storage libraries may involve libraries of different types as in the case of the New England Deposit Library. Cooperative photographic projects such as the one between the Library of Congress and the University of North Carolina which is preparing microfilms of early state records of the American colonies is another area. The main stress is on cooperation between academic libraries. A bibliography is included.

109. Hanke, Kate G. "Public Library—School Cooperation," *Wilson Library Bulletin* 30: 626-27 (April 1956).

To keep children reading when they have no access to branch libraries during the summer, Austin (Tex.) initiated a project using a school library as a branch. The school library was stocked with materials from the public library, an experienced bookmobile librarian assigned to direct it, and a group of children active in the school library program enlisted as helpers. The project was reported as a success.

110. Dunningham, A. G. W. "National and State Library Development," *New Zealand Libraries* 19: 57-70 (April-May 1956) and 19: 93-97 (June 1956).

The New Zealand Library Association and the National Library Service have developed a national library system for their country. This system has achieved cooperation between public, university, and special libraries. There is a good deal of interlibrary lending in New Zealand and there is also a union list of serials. The main concern of the article is the extension of public library service through district or regional systems. The author reviews various methods of regional library service in the United States, Canada, and other countries. New Zealand has not yet achieved complete library service to the counties of New Zealand and consequently library service to rural areas is inadequate.

111. Edwards, Lon. "Public Library and Schools Can Cooperate," *School and Community* 42: 14, 19 (May 1956).

The North Kansas City Public Library and the public schools in the area are building a strong reading program through library visits and education in the use of library tools.

112. Wand, M. W. "References and Information Services in County Libraries," *Librarian and Book World* 45: 94-97 (May-June 1956).

The head of Reference Services of the Middlesex County Library (England) briefly describes the development of reference service in county libraries with examples of developments in several counties. One of the examples is Hertfordshire in which the libraries of the County Technical Colleges are integrated with the County Library Service. Technical colleges circulate copies of periodicals and abstracts among local firms and provide information service to industry. A union catalog of periodical holdings in public and special libraries has been compiled, and new books purchased by all libraries are entered in a county library catalog.

113. Mahoney, Orcena. "Cooperation in Processing," *Missouri Library Association Quarterly* 18: 63-65 (June 1956).

Reference is made in this article to several examples of centralized processing. In Norway centralized cataloging is tied to centralized purchasing for state-aided school and rural public libraries. In Germany some dozen university, research, state, and large public libraries have combined in acquisition of materials, formation of a union catalog, and interlibrary lending. For the United States, Georgia's centralized system of catalog card distribution is given as an example.

114. Kusel, Mary A. "School-Community Center-Library," *Texas Libraries* 18: 155-57 (Oct. 1956).

A cooperative agreement between the London Independent School, a rural school southwest of Corpus Christi, and the Nueces County (Tex.) Library was reached in which the county library agreed to provide all the technical services required to organize a school library and to instruct the school personnel in running the library. In return the school provided space for an adult collection and agreed to supervise its circulation. This joint arrangement provides the children with a school library and adults in the rural area with a book collection.

115. "School and Public Library Cooperation," *New Mexico Library Bulletin* 20: 6 (Oct. 1956).

This article relates how the librarian of Gadsden (N. Mex.) High School aided a group of local women in the establishment of a public library in Anthony. Help was given in instruction in library procedure, and in accessioning and cataloging a small collection of books.

116. Drewry, Virginia. "Central Cataloging on the State Level in Georgia," *PLD Reporter* 5: 42-44 (Nov. 1956).

In Georgia there is a plan through which school and public libraries may purchase library materials and catalog cards through a central office in the Division of Instructional Materials and Library Service of the State Department of Education. The service is used by regional library systems, county libraries, and elementary and high school libraries.

117. "Significant Library Development Project," *Bookmark* 9: 47-48 (Dec. 1956).

The Library Development Project of the Pacific Northwest Library Association is conducting its investigation over a two-year period ending 30 June 1958. The aim of the project is to study the library resources of the area with a view toward eventual cooperation and sharing of resources among the libraries in the region. The Library Development Project is organized into four major divisions dealing with (1) public libraries; (2) college, university, and special libraries; (3) elementary and secondary school libraries; and (4) a synthesis of all library activities in the region.

1957

118. Hughesdon, Harold, and Costello, Gertrude. "An Experiment in Cooperation," *ALA Bulletin* 51: 129-33 (Feb. 1957).

The creation of the union list of serials, *Periodical Holdings and Subscriptions in Eight Minnesota Libraries,* by six colleges in the St. Paul area plus the St. Paul Public Library and the Hill Reference Library is described here. The union list is intended to serve as a device for cooperative storage, selection of new titles, exchange of duplicates, and the discard of duplicates rather than as a finding list. In addition to this activity, copies of the classed catalog of the Hill Reference Library have been placed in the college libraries and in the St. Paul Public Library. Other areas in which future cooperation is being considered are also discussed.

119. Newhouse, Jeanne, and Watts, Doris Ryder. "Planning Together—School Library and Public Library, Who Should Take the Initiative," *Top of the News* 13: 27-31 (March 1957).

This article describes the cooperation between the high school librarian and the public librarian to interest Long Beach (Calif.) youth in using libraries by providing combined service in answering school assignment needs. Jointly sponsored book reviews and reading groups acquaint students with new areas of interest for pleasure reading.

120. Rates, R. D. "Co-operative Industrial and Commercial Reference and Information Service," *Aslib Proceedings* 9: 83-84 (March 1957).

The Commercial and Technical Library Service (CICRIS, West London) began in 1951 "in order to provide a convenient source of information to every firm that needs it." At the present time 64 business firms are served mainly through the resources in ten public libraries and their branches. Each public library system specializes in certain technologies while five of the public libraries maintain union lists of basic types of materials which are of value to the participating firms.

121. Gosnell, Charles E. "The Collection," *Library Trends* 6: 28-34 (July 1957).

The New York State Library provides extensive service to other libraries in the state. It is unique since its primary responsibility is to serve college, public, and special libraries through loan of expensive, rare, and infrequently used materials. The New York service, regarded as one form of state subsidy, encourages local libraries to discard little-used material with the assurance that, when needed, such works may be secured from Albany.

122. Roedde, W. A. "The Northwestern Regional Library Cooperation," *Ontario Library Review* 41: 205-6 (Aug. 1957).

The Northwestern Regional Library serves 120 libraries and schools in the district of Rainy River and Thunder Bay in northwestern Ontario and will in time serve the vast Kenora-Patricia district with an additional 153,000 square miles. The library began in 1953 as an experiment sponsored by Angus Mowat, Ontario's Director of Public Library Service.

123. Edson, Miriam M. "Programming and Scheduling School Bookmobile Service," *ALA Bulletin* 51: 695-702 (Oct. 1957).

The service and functioning of the Lucas County (Ohio) Library bookmobile system to 37 schools in Lucas County is the concern of this article. Cooperation between teachers and librarians to more adequately meet the needs of the students is described. Information on scheduling, staffing and facilities is included.

124. Amorin, Maria Jose Theresa de. "Cooperative Cataloging in Brazil," *Library Resources and Technical Services* 1: 35-39 (Winter 1957).

Servicio de Intercambio de Catalogacao (SIC) was established in 1942 by the Brazilian Administrative Department of Public Service (DASP). Although it was originally established as an independent organization operating as a cataloging exchange service, it later became a department of the Brazilian Institute for Bibliography and Documentation. Initial participants of SIC were the Machado de Assis Library and the governmental libraries of the Administrative Department of Public Service, of the then Ministry of Health, Education, and Welfare, of the National Museum, of the General Treasury Office, and of the National Department of Printing. The current number of cooperating libraries is 120.

Tasks of SIC consist of much the same responsibilities as the Library of Congress, that is, to provide uniform catalog cards to its participant members. Catalog cards are sent to SIC by member libraries to be checked and printed in uniformity with other Brazilian libraries. Cards are then returned to the cooperating libraries.

1958

125. Grazier, Robert T. "Cooperation Among Libraries of Different Types," *Library Trends* 6: 331-42 (Jan. 1958).

Grazier considers some of the different types of cooperative activities, the administrative arrangements used, and some of the difficulties encountered. The exchange of information about acquisitions and holdings is one of the more common activities, and the Philadelphia Union Library Catalog is described as an example of this type. Cooperative efforts which have failed, such as the Omaha Union Catalog of Chemistry Information, are also discussed.

The exchange of catalog cards as a means of enlarging access to community resources has been used by some libraries either for all current acquisitions or for acquisitions in a specific subject area, as between the Art and Architecture Library of Washington University and the St. Louis City Art Museum. Union lists are described, e.g., the *Worcester Union List of Serials, North Texas Union List of Serials,* and *A Union List of Serials in the Washington University Libraries and the Henry Shaw Botanical Garden Library and the Library of Monsanto Chemical Company.*

Problems in the area of cooperative book acquisitions are discussed and several examples of successful programs are given. Four libraries in the Houston area have worked out such a plan, and the Detroit Public Library and Wayne State University exchange information about microtext publications. Another such project mentioned is the cooperative acquisitions policy of the Chicago Public, John Crerar, and Newberry Libraries. Seven libraries in the Baltimore area have an agreement covering the purchase of historical manuscripts, genealogy, and archives of Maryland and Baltimore. The Cleveland Public Library purchases the Evans microprint project and Western Reserve obtains the titles in the *Short-Title Catalog* in microfilm editions.

Agreements covering the exchange of duplicate or unwanted materials exist in a number of cases. The Milwaukee Public Library and the Milwaukee Special Libraries Chapter have an agreement of this kind. In other instances special collections have been transferred to libraries with existing specialized collections. The Academy of Natural Sciences of Philadelphia transferred material to the American Philosophical Society, and the University of Pennsylvania transferred its material on horology to Franklin Institute. Interlibrary loan service among area libraries is common. Syracuse University and the special libraries in the area have agreements which permit joint use of materials by faculty and staff. In Colorado the State Board of Examiners for Professional Engineers and Land Surveyors and the Colorado State Board of Examiners for Architects gave their libraries to the Denver Public Library. In addition the two boards make an annual grant to the public library for the purchase of materials in their areas of interest.

The sections on the administrative machinery of cooperative projects and on the types of projects which succeed and why will be of interest to anyone considering a cooperative project.

126. Ley, Ronald. "Relation of the Regional Library to the School," *British Columbia Quarterly* 21: 31-33 (Jan. 1958).

Since 1939 the Fraser Valley Regional Library (British Columbia) has assisted in serving elementary school libraries. The Okanagan and Vancouver Island Regional Libraries serve both elementary and secondary schools, classroom talks and talks to the PTA's are given by the children's librarian, and bulletins of library information are circulated to teachers. Summer Leisure Reading Clubs have also been organized.

127. Stanford, Edward B. "Increasing Library Resources Through Cooperation," *Library Trends* 6: 296-308 (Jan. 1958).

Stanford writes of the reliance of the University of Minnesota on the Minnesota Historical Library for holdings in local histories, and for Minnesota manuscript and newspaper collections.

128. "Interlibrary Center at Chapel Hill: Report of the Cooperative Library Resources Committee," *North Carolina Libraries* 16: 50-51 (Feb. 1958).

A committee charged with investigating expansion and utilization of the union catalog of North Carolina libraries and faciliting interlibrary loans among the state's college, public, school, special, and university libraries made a series of recommendations in 1958 which were later approved by the University Board and the State Library. There were six main points to the program proposed:

- The North Carolina Union Catalog at the University of North Carolina was to be expanded with listings of significant holdings in other North Carolina libraries; the North Carolina State Library would continue to build a union catalog of resources in other state agencies in Raleigh and the significant holdings in public libraries
- Interlibrary loan sources at the university library will be brought together, and those requests which lie in the operational sphere of the state library will be relayed to it; the state library will relay to the university library any requests beyond its ability to serve
- Each of these two libraries will handle basic reference requests and refer those requiring specialized resources to the appropriate place
- Direct wire communication between the state library and the university library with other libraries invited to tie in
- Personnel would come from present staffs with some expansion from the requested grant
- Physical needs were to be supplied by the university.

129. Tolman, Mason. "The Literature of Science and the Library," *Library Journal* 83: 1360-62 (1 May 1958).

Tolman describes the efforts of the New York State Library to strengthen its science collection. A printed catalog is in preparation to facilitate interlibrary lending of these materials to all libraries throughout the state.

130. Adcock, Elizabeth. "Centralized Technical Processes in a County Library," *Library Resources and Technical Services* 2: 191-95 (Summer 1958).

The Weld County Library (Greeley, Colo.) established the Centralized Purchasing and Processing project in 1955 to help the school libraries meet accreditation standards. The plan has worked satisfactorily for three years. In 1957 about 2,000 new books were ordered and processed for schools and public libraries in the county. The six small public libraries in the county have been slow to participate, but the school libraries have been "most enthusiastic on the basis of increased economy, more accurate cataloging, and especially more released time for the teacher-librarian to give other library service."

131. Drewry, Virginia. "Georgia State Catalog Card Service," *Library Resources and Technical Services* 2: 176-80 (Summer 1958).

A centralized catalog card service is part of Georgia's program of state aid to school and public libraries. Operating within the Division of Instructional Materials and Library Services Division of the State Department of Education, it served 30 regional libraries, 49 county libraries and 772 individual schools in 1958. The program is financed by state funds, and furnishes catalog cards at a minimal cost of 5¢ per set. The format of the cards, the supervisory staff, and developments in the program since its establishment in 1944 are discussed.

132. Haugh, W. S. "The Public Library and the School Library: 1, Bristol," *School Librarian* 9: 101-4 (July 1958).

In Bristol (England) a School Library Service was established in 1954. A collection of books is housed at one of the branch libraries and teachers make selections from the collection for their schools. Special attention is given to the 7-10 year old group; it is felt that older children can more easily visit the public libraries if they are making some sort of special study.

133. Ahlers, Eleanor E. "School and Public Library Cooperation," *Mountain-Plains Library Quarterly* 3: 9-12 (Fall 1958).

Many specific examples of school-public library cooperation in various parts of the country are mentioned here. Much of the same material may also be found in Ahlers, Eleanor E. "School and Public Library Cooperation: Standards, Goals—Now What?" *Ohio Library Association Bulletin* 30: 15-20 (Jan. 1960), and Ahlers, Eleanor E. "School and Public Library Cooperation," *Montana Library Quarterly* 4: 3-9 (July 1959).

134. Butler, Joan. "The Public Library and the School Library: 2, Hertfordshire," *School Librarian* 9: 188-93 (Dec. 1958).

An explanation of the ways in which the county library helps the schools in Hertfordshire (England). There is a loan service to all schools to supplement their own school libraries. "An exhibition collection of books suitable for school libraries is maintained at headquarters so that teachers may examine books when building up their library stocks." The county library gives advice on cataloging and classification, furniture, and general administration of the school library. Many other areas of cooperation are described also.

1959

135. Jackson, William V. "The Specifics of Interlibrary Organization," in Rose B. Phelps, and Janet Phillips, eds., *The Library as a Community Information Center,* p.36-50. (Allerton Park Institute, no.4) Champaign, Ill.: Illini Union Book Store, 1959.

Jackson discusses the importance of union lists, union catalogs, and guides to resources as forms of interlibrary cooperation and as the basis for interlibrary lending. The background and scope of some of the national and regional union projects, some of them involving different types of libraries are given, along with some of the problems and costs involved. The author points out some of the advantages of union lists and some of the requirements for successful cooperative projects.

136. Great Britain. Ministry of Education. *The Structure of the Public Library Service in England and Wales; Report of the Committee Appointed by the Minister of Education in September 1957.* London: H.M.S.O., 1959. 57p.

This report (Roberts Report) is concerned primarily with the structure of public library service in England and Wales and with recommendations for change. A brief description is given of the ten regional library bureaus, whose primary purpose is to serve as agencies through which public libraries can borrow from each other. The bureaus also maintain union catalogs of books in the constituent libraries that form the basis of a National Union Catalog at the National Central Library. The most common cooperative practice is interlibrary lending. Among the recommendations of the study are that the existing regional committees be given statutory recognition within their regions and that they work with the National Central Library in providing a national system of cooperation. The regional bureaus would also be required to outline schemes showing the organization and scope of the arrangements for cooperation and what provisions will be made for the cost of the work.

137. Adcock, Elizabeth. "County Library Sells Technical Processing to School Libraries," *ALA Bulletin* 53: 128 (Feb. 1959).

The Weld County Library (Greeley, Col.) provides a central purchasing and processing plan designed to help school libraries meet accreditation and give teacher-librarians more time with their students. In 1958, twenty-four school libraries representing sixteen school systems and two public libraries were participants.

Each year an exhibit of books is provided with a grading scale and teachers, librarians, and administrators select the books they wish to order. Wilson printed cards are used, and the county library takes charge of arranging a catalog and shelf list and delivering the materials.

For these services, the school pays the cost of the book, supplies, clerical labor, and a 5¢ charge.

138. Estabrooks, Edith E. "How Not to Give Bookmobile Service to Schools," *ALA Bulletin* 53: 129-30 (Feb. 1959).

The Tri-County Library Services Center (Bridgeton, N.J.), the schools, and community organizations cooperate in a campaign to develop bookmobile service for the community at large and not limited only to school children.

139. Taylor, Helene Scherff. "A Public Library Discontinues School Services," *ALA Bulletin* 53: 125-26 (Feb. 1959).

A survey of public library service to elementary schools in Bloomfield (N.J.) led the library trustees to decide to discontinue service to the elementary schools. Service had included branches or deposit stations in the schools, serviced by public library personnel. The Board of Education assumed maintenance of elementary school libraries. The public library was concerned about the drain on its financial resources and the duplication of service.

140. Bard, Harriet E. "More Can be Accomplished by Cooperation," *Indiana School Librarians' Association's News Noser* 13: 4-5 (March 1959).

A detailed step-by-step description of the process by which Morrison-Reeves Public Library in Richmond (Ind.) catalogs books for six elementary schools in Richmond and Wayne Townships.

141. Birkelund, Palle. "The Danish Bibliographical Office," *Library Journal* 84: 708-11 (1 March 1959).

All Danish libraries are parts of a common library system, and there is good cooperation between different types of libraries. The entire library system is divided into public libraries and research libraries. There is a good deal of interlibrary lending between the two groups. The Danish Bibliographical Bureau is the "cornerstone" of Danish libraries. The bureau carries on such activities as centralized cataloging and distribution of printed catalog cards for Danish books, preparation of the Danish national bibliography (*Dansk Bogfortegnelse*), publication of an *Index of Danish Periodicals (Dansk Tidsskriftindex),* and the *Index of Articles in Danish Newspapers (Aviskronikindex)* and many other activities which are detailed in the article.

142. "The Public Library and the School Library: Four Articles," *Canadian Library* 15: 209-14 (March 1959).

Here are four short essays on cooperation between public libraries and schools as it existed in 1959. The articles included are: "The School and the Small Library," by A. W. Bowron; "Toronto: Libraries in Elementary Schools," by Winifred Davis; "Vancouver: School Libraries," by Muriel Carruthers; and "Vancouver Island: Regional Library Service to Schools," by C. K. Morison.

143. Fuller, Helen. "Public Library Service to Elementary Schools in Long Beach," *ALA Bulletin* 53: 303-4 (April 1959).

As part of a vacation reading program the Long Beach (Calif.) Public Library prepares reading lists at various levels and distributes them to teachers. The teachers select a reading list at an appropriate level for each child and send it home with the child's report card on the last day of school.

144. Phipps, Mildred R. "Public Library Service to Elementary Schools in Pasadena," *ALA Bulletin* 53: 304-5 (April 1959).

This is a description of how elementary schools without libraries are served by the public library and its branches in Pasadena (Calif.).

145. Sass, Samuel. "Must Special Libraries be Parasites?" *Special Libraries* 1: 149-54 (April 1959). Reprinted in Harold S. Sharp, ed., *Readings in Special Librarianship,* p.301-15. New York: Scarecrow Pr., 1963.

The author contends that special libraries are parasitic in that they borrow far more materials from larger college and public libraries than they lend. He urges special libraries to take advantage of the specialized collections of other special libraries and discusses a survey he made from which he concluded that very little cooperation between special libraries and other types exists. Numerous instances of interlibrary cooperation are mentioned in passing. Cooperation was found to be exceptionally good in Hartford (Conn.), Wilmington (Del.), and Kalamazoo (Mich.). Industrial libraries contribute to the following bibliographical centers: the North Carolina Union Catalog, Cleveland Regional Catalog, the Nebraska Union Catalog, the Union Catalog of the Atlanta-Athens Area, and the Philadelphia Bibliographical Center. The Philadelphia Center serves about 100 industrial firms and lists the holdings of 13 industrial libraries.

146. *Working Together, Some Aspects of Library Co-operation.* Papers read at the Week-end Conference of the London and Home Counties Branch of the Library Association held at Clacton-on-Sea, 10th-12th April 1959. London: The Library Assn., 1959. 75p.

The state of the art of library cooperation in Great Britain in 1959 is the subject of this pamphlet. There are articles on "The National Interlending System," "Library Cooperation: London Area," and "The Supply of Books to University Students." Included is an article by Edward Dudley on the Commercial and Technical Library Service, West London (CICRIS). This organization encourages cooperation between special libraries and public libraries with emphasis on speedy access to needed materials.

147. Boord, Miller. "A University Cooperates," *Wilson Library Bulletin* 33: 651, 684 (May 1959).

Boord explains how Southern Illinois University helped to extend library service to the rural areas of southern Illinois in the late 1950s.

148. Harris, Katherine G. "The Joint Acquisitions Committee of the Detroit Public Library and Wayne State University Library," *Stechert-Hafner Book News* 13: 109-11 (May 1959).

In 1957 a Joint Acquisitions Committee was established by the Wayne State University Libraries and the Detroit Public Library. The purpose of the committee was to review the acquisitions policies of both libraries in the hope that an analysis of the collections in these neighboring libraries would provide some insight into a more proficient method of cooperative acquisitions between them. After a partial examination of the collections in each library, the committee recommended that both libraries continue to collect in areas which are of particular interest to their respective patrons. However, materials in the following categories should be considered as materials to be shared between the libraries:

- Expensive (over $100) in-print or out-of-print items
- Continuations and periodicals of limited or specialized use, both current and back files
- Microprint or microfilm projects which are expensive initially or involve expense over a period of years
- Major publishing projects, particularly foreign ones
- Specialized indexes, bibliographies, and other tools.
- Esoteric and potentially little-used materials.

149. Trotier, Arnold H. "Cataloging in Source: The Story up to Now," *Illinois Libraries* 41: 426-31 (June 1959).

Trotier reports on preparations for a survey to measure the use made of catalog entries prepared under the "cataloging in source" experiment, the speed of processing publications for use, the cost of cataloging, and methods used to transfer catalog entries from books to cards.

150. Parrott, F. P. "The Public Library and the School Library: Reading," *School Librarian* 9: 361-62 (July 1959).

The history of cooperation between the Reading (England) Public Library and the schools of Reading from 1889 to 1959 is described, with a final paragraph on cooperation in 1959.

151. Workshop for School and Public Librarians, Trustees, and Administrators. 17-21 August 1959. *Proceedings,* p.30. Sponsored by Arkansas Library Association and Arkansas Library Commission with the cooperation of University of Arkansas and State Department of Education. Fayetteville, Ark.: The Workshop Sponsors, 1959.

A cooperative book fair program sponsored by the public library, the college library, and the schools in the area of the Faulkner-Van Buren Regional Library (Ark.) is described.

152. Boord, Miller. "Southern Illinois Regional Library, Carbondale," *Illinois Libraries* 41: 502-3 (Sept. 1959).

In 1959 the Illinois State Library and Southern Illinois University cosponsored the Southern Illinois Regional Library at Carbondale. Under this Federal Library Services Act project, 34 counties in southern Illinois were served. Between 1957 and 1959 a bookmobile service served 31 public libraries in 21 counties. An annual Public Library Institute and an annual Library Trustees' Conference was held at Southern Illinois University for 34 counties in southern Illinois.

153. "A Cooperative Acquisitions Program. Wayne State University and the Detroit Public Library," Detroit Public Library. *Among Friends* 16: 1-2 (Fall 1959).

The cooperative acquisitions program was adopted by the Detroit Public Library and the libraries of Wayne State University in 1957. The program provides for the purchasing of expensive publications which are of primary importance to the library resources of the area but which are too specialized for inclusion in both libraries. The responsibility for these items is divided between the two libraries based on the various fields of specialization within the respective libraries. The most recent undertaking of the program provided for the acquisition of numerous periodical titles in the fields of computation and automation. After certain titles considered necessary to the welfare of each library had been agreed upon, a considerable number of other titles were cooperatively selected and added to the library collections.

154. Smith, Hannis S. "The Case for Independent School Libraries," *American School Board Journal* 139: 23-24 (Oct. 1959).

This article explains why public libraries are discontinuing branch libraries in schools in Minneapolis and Madison and why there should be independent school libraries. The author states that the experiment of combined school-public libraries failed because "neither library could do a good job of serving its proper public."

155. Ferguson, Elizabeth. "Special Libraries Need Not be Parasites," *Library Journal* 84: 3372-75 (1 Nov. 1959).

Elizabeth Ferguson believes that special libraries can play an important part in the interchange of information in a community. Informal, but practical, cooperation does exist between special libraries and universities and special libraries and public libraries. The Greensboro (N.C.) Public Library contacted area business and industrial firms and asked the firms if their libraries would make material available to other firms or individuals if the Greensboro Public Library would act as middleman. Since then, there has been some use of the exchange facilities.

156. Dale, N. A. "The Public Library and the School Library: 4, Lancashire," *School Librarian* 9: 441-44 (Dec. 1959).

The book sharing policies of the Lancashire County (England) Public Library with the area's schools is described. Better methods of selecting, processing, and guiding reading have resulted from this cooperative system.

1960

157. Drennan, Henry T., and Wenberg, Louise T. "School-Public Relations," in Morton Kroll, ed., Pacific Northwest Library Association. Library Development Project Reports, v.2. *Elementary and Secondary School Libraries of the Pacific Northwest*, p.248-301. Seattle: Univ. of Washington Pr., 1960.

This paper surveys the informal relationship which has existed between public libraries and schools in the region and notes the changes in services provided to the schools by the public libraries. The authors point out the need for improved communication between the two agencies and make recommendations for improvements in both school library service and children's services in the public libraries.

Public librarians and school administrators were asked to evaluate the relationship between the schools and the public libraries. School administrators in metropolitan areas were unsure of what the relationship should be. In smaller places heavy reliance was placed on the public library by the schools, and in rural areas school administrators were content to accept book service from the public library.

Public librarians in metropolitan areas are withdrawing classroom collection service, despite doubts about the schools' interest in establishing school libraries. In smaller towns and rural areas public librarians express considerable doubt about the ability of school personnel to establish library service in the individual schools. There is also some feeling about maintaining service to schools as a means of presenting the public library to the children.

Other findings indicated that there was virtually no professional consultation between public and school librarians.

Recommendations included in the study were aimed at strengthening library service in the schools, improving children's services in the public libraries, increasing the number of reference personnel and materials to meet the needs of students at the public library, and improving salaries and preparation for people in children's work. State agencies are also called on to give attention to the problems of professional consultation and communication at the local level.

158. Skipper, James E. "Library Cooperation in Metropolitan New York," in Keyes D. Metcalf, dir., *Studies in Library Administrative Problems; Eight Reports from a Seminar in Library Administration,* p.77-94. New Brunswick, N.J.: Rutgers Univ. Pr., 1960.

This study deals with interlibrary cooperation and is restricted to the Reference Department of the New York Public Library, Columbia University Library, and the subject areas of law, medicine, and engineering.

The report discusses the problems and possibilities for cooperation in acquisitions, cataloging, use, transfer of collections, and storage. Recommendations in the areas of use, acquisitions, and storage include freer access to certain specialized collections at Columbia and the New York Public Library. Cooperative acquisitions programs in college catalogs, house organs, foreign law, and the publications of regulatory commissions are recommended.

Appendixes list past cooperative efforts in acquisitions, cooperative cataloging, use, transfer of collections, and cooperative storage.

Since completion of the study a small staff has been appointed to the offices of the Council of Higher Educational Institutions in New York City to study the problem and try to find ways and means to promote interlibrary cooperation.

159. Blasingame, Ralph. "Cooperation Between the Pennsylvania State Library and the Union Library Catalog," *Pennsylvania Library Association Bulletin* 15: 67-68 (Winter 1960).

In 1959-60 a program was established to forward to the Union Library Catalog of the Philadelphia Metropolitan Area any interlibrary loan requests that could not be filled at the Pennsylvania State Library.

160. Carnovsky, Leon. "The St. Paul Public Library and the James Jerome Hill Reference Library: A Study of Cooperative Possibilities." [St. Paul: St. Paul Public Library] Jan. 1960. 41*l*. Mimeographed.

The James Jerome Hill Reference Library and the St. Paul (Minn.) Public Library are located in the same building but are administered separately. This survey reports on the cooperation in subject specialization that has existed and gives suggestions for further division in acquisitions between the two libraries and other libraries in the Twin Cities. A cooperative storage center for the back files of periodicals for all the libraries in the metropolitan area is also recommended.

161. "Cooperation Between Public and School Libraries to Gain Better Public Service," *Iowa Library Quarterly* 18: 166-69 (Jan. 1960).

This article is a report of a talk by Sidney P. Marland, Superintendent of Public Schools of Winnetka, Illinois. He feels that school and public libraries not only should be separate, but that children need libraries separate and distinct from the schools.

The author cites an instance in Evanston (Ill.) in which the removal of a public library branch from a school to a shopping center resulted in a sharp increase in circulation. He also cites a Salt Lake City cost study of independent and school-housed public library branches which indicated that school-housed branches are more expensive to operate.

There is additional discussion of the essentials of a school library.

162. Bebbington, John. "Twenty-seven Years of Cooperation with Industry," *Librarian and Book World* 29: 21-26 (Feb. 1960).

Bebbington gives a description of the Sheffield (England) Interchange Organization (SINTO), a cooperative arrangement first organized in 1933, involving the city library, the University Library and the Applied Service Library, the Chamber of Commerce, nine research associations and similar institutions, and 36 industrial organizations.

Under the general administration of the city librarian, the organization pools materials in a partial union catalog of books and a union list of serials and makes them available to members through lending or the provision of photocopies. Both mail and messenger service are provided.

The article describes procedures used in locating items and filling requests and for the maintenance of the union lists. Other activities related to the sponsorship of conferences and special projects are also described.

163. Kingery, Robert E. "Latin American Cooperative Acquisitions Project," *Stechert-Hafner Book News* 14: 65-66 (Feb. 1960).

The history of the joint agreement between the University of Texas, the New York Public Library, and Stechert-Hafner in launching the Latin

American Cooperative Acquisitions Project (LACAP) to improve the coverage of Latin American imprints by research libraries in the United States is detailed by Mr. Kingery.

164. Microfilming Clearing House Bulletin no.71. An appendix to *Library of Congress Information Bulletin* 19: 107-10 (29 Feb. 1960).

A wealth of information on all types of cooperative microfilm projects is presented here. The New York Public Library, in cooperation with the United Nations Library, is filming the official gazettes of Latin American countries. The New York Public Library also has a program with University Microfilms, Inc., for an efficient program of microfilming current Congressional hearings. The Historical Society of Delaware and the Longwood Library of Kennett Square (Pa.) have microfilmed selected Delaware newspapers for the period 1800-1835.

165. "Report from Dr. Benson and LACAP," *Stechert-Hafner Book News* 14: 80 (March 1960).

A report from Dr. Nettie L. Benson on the first trip to Latin America in behalf of the Latin American Acquisitions Project. Types of materials sought and difficulties in obtaining them are described.

166. Taylor, Mark. "Liaison Through Workshops," *Library Journal* 85: 3164-66 (15 Sept. 1960).

Dayton and Montgomery County Public Library held two workshops with public librarians, school librarians, and school English teachers to discuss problems of serving school children in the public library. Suggestions for conducting successful workshops are included.

167. Paulin, L. V. "Technical Library Services," in *Proceedings, Papers, and Summaries of Discussions at the Scarborough Conference, 13th to 16th September 1960,* p.59-67. London: The Library Assn., 1960.

The provision by libraries of technical books, periodicals, and information to business and industry is widespread in England. Paulin describes five cooperative organizations based in large municipal libraries, but operating with libraries of all types. Interlibrary lending and the maintenance of union lists and catalogs are the most common activities.

The Tyneside Association of Libraries for Industry and Commerce (TALIC) based in Newcastle includes 48 municipal, county, university, technical college, and industrial libraries which provide service to firms without charge, unless photocopies are requested.

The Liverpool and District Scientific Industrial and Research Libraries Advisory Council (LADSIRLAC) provides service at two levels on a subscription basis. The lesser rate provides the subscriber with a monthly Documents Bulletin, literature searches, limited borrowing privileges and a monthly list of new books; the higher rate permits unrestricted borrowing, access to a translation index, literature searches and answers to inquiries.

The article also describes what certain counties are doing in the provision of technical information, either through technical colleges or county libraries.

The other organizations discussed are Cooperative Industrial Reference and Information Service (CICRIS), Sheffield Interchange Organization (SINTO), and Huddersfield and District Information Scheme (HADIS).

168. Urquhart, D. J. "The National Lending Library for Science and Technology, in *Proceedings, Papers and Summaries of Discussions at the Scarborough Conference, 13th to 16th September 1960,* p.51-57. London: The Library Assn., 1960.

A discussion of the plans for the creation of the National Lending Library for Science and Technology (N.L.L.), at Boston Spa in West Riding (England) is presented. The purpose is to provide the practitioner in science or technology with all the literature of the world he may need. The scope of the collection, the service to be provided, and the place of the library in the country's interlibrary loan scheme are described in some detail.

169. "Heard at Our Northeast Harbor Meeting." *Bulletin of the Maine Library Association* 21: 9-13 (Nov. 1960).

Summaries of two discussions that took place at a meeting of the Maine Library Association are given here. One discussion concerned cooperation between school and public librarians, and many examples are given and suggestions made on such topics as cooperative book selection. The second discussion was on "cooperative purchase and storage of books" and urged cooperation between different types of libraries in Maine.

1961

170. Metcalf, Keyes D. *Cooperation Among Maine Libraries; A Report Prepared for the Larger Libraries of Maine.* Cambridge, Mass.: The Author, 1961. 22p.

Seven libraries in Maine (Bates College, Colby College, Bowdoin, University of Maine, the Bangor and Portland Public Libraries, and the Maine State Library) had met informally for some years to discuss various aspects of interlibrary cooperation. This survey was undertaken to explore areas in which programs of cooperation might be established. Joint storage, bibliographical control, and interlibrary use are among the general areas considered. Cooperative acquisitions in serials, public documents, microproductions, and Maine materials is urged. Interlibrary use suggestions include a search form for unlocated materials, photographic reproduction equipment, and arrangements with outside libraries for interlibrary loan on a contract basis.

171. Eckford, Mary Lathrop, "Library Service Center of Eastern Ohio; an Experiment in Centralized Processing," *Library Resources and Technical Services* 5: 5-40 (Winter 1961).

A centralized processing center serves 17 public libraries and 18 public schools in eastern Ohio. A committee from the membership developed a common set of cataloging practices which had been used for two years without change.

172. Esterquest, Ralph T. "Cooperation in Library Services," *Library Quarterly* 31: 71-89 (Jan. 1961).

This paper presents a survey of attempts at library cooperation and summarizes some of the trends visible in the period from the 1930s through the 1950s. The author presents a definition of library cooperation and reviews examples of cooperation in 12 different areas including union lists, cooperative acquisitions, cooperative storage, and bibliographical centers. He also discusses the difficulty of evaluating cooperative projects and some of the problems faced when such projects are undertaken. Five areas for further effort are listed.

While not specifically concerned with cooperation among different types of libraries, the paper deals with some of the assumptions underlying most cooperative efforts.

173. Hopkinson, Shirley L. "Centralized Cataloging and Indexing Services," *Library Journal* 86: 747-49 (15 Feb. 1961).

"The present and probable future trends in centralized cataloging and indexing services among California libraries were explored by a panel of practicing librarians at a recent institute sponsored by the Department of Librarianship of San Jose State College." Panel members included librarians from a special library, three school district central libraries and a county library.

Cooperation between libraries and library systems in ordering and processing of materials has already begun. Some county libraries permit school libraries in their areas to join their cataloging service.

174. "Cooperative Planning for Public Libraries: An Institute Sponsored by the School of Library Science, University of Southern California, Thursday-Friday, February 16-17, 1961," *News Notes of California Libraries* 56, pt.2: 214-86 (Spring 1961).

This issue is given over to the papers presented at the Institute on Cooperative Planning for Public Libraries sponsored by the School of Library Science of the University of Southern California in 1961. The purpose of the conference was to explore the possibility of the establishment in southern California of a bibliographic center and reference centers. One of the articles explores "examples of some successful bibliographical centers." Most of the papers considered the problems which could be solved by the establishment of a bibliographic center and reference centers.

175. Hoskin, Beryl. "Library Cooperation in Santa Clara," *California Librarian* 22: 79-85 (April 1961).

The public library is at the center of cooperation in Santa Clara (Calif.); its program includes "visits throughout the school year to all the schools, guest cards to all the teachers, book talks and general speeches to the P.T.A. and Parents' Guilds . . . a summer reading program, informal classes in the teaching and use of the library to school children, and interlibrary loans to the school libraries and the University Library." The Library of the University of Santa Clara lends books to other libraries in town on request and high school students in accelerated groups can also use the library. The teachers of the schools are trying to work closely with public librarians by giving the library a warning on upcoming research projects and requesting purchase of books that might be helpful to students.

176. Kaser, David. "The Interdependence of Academic Libraries," *Kentucky Library Association Bulletin* 15: 3-9 (April 1961).

The John Crerar Library and the Newberry Library in Chicago have worked out a plan for distributing the responsibility for collecting research materials in the fields of science and technology and the humanities. Newberry will continue to collect primarily in the field of humanities while the Crerar Library will be solely responsible for the fields of the sciences and technology. The Chicago Public Library has been assigned the responsibility of collecting extensively in the area of general literature as well as in several special classes of materials including architecture, documents, newspapers, and patents.

177. Binns, Norman E. "Cooperative Schemes of Library Service for Industry and Commerce," *Unesco Bulletin for Libraries* 15: 311-16 (Nov.-Dec. 1961).

Binns describes a number of schemes for providing library service to commerce and industry now operating in Britain and Europe. Sheffield Interchange Organization (SINTO) has operated since 1933 and has over 50 members drawn from all types of libraries in the area. Co-operative Industrial and Commercial Reference and Information Service (CICRIS) was founded in 1951 to serve the London area. Acton Public Library serves as headquarters for CICRIS, which has over 80 active members drawn from county libraries, borough libraries, technical libraries, and industrial libraries. Hull Technical Interloan Scheme (HULTIS), founded in 1953 with headquarters in the Hull City Library, now has a membership of over 35 firms and institutions. Liverpool and District Scientific Industrial and Research Libraries Advisory Council (LADSIRLAC) was inaugurated in 1956 and is based on the resources of a large city reference library. Tyneside Association of Libraries for Industry and Commerce (TALIC), founded in 1958, has a membership consisting of public, university, and institutional libraries and commercial and industrial firms. The most recent scheme of this type is the Hertfordshire Technical Library and Information Service (1961) through which the entire resources of the county library and many academic libraries are made available to industry in the area. In addition, services of this type are planned for Southampton, Nottingham, Burnley, Huddersfield, Chelmsford, and Thurrock. Similar cooperation has been proposed in the United States between Enoch Pratt Free Library, the Center for Documentation Research at Western Reserve University, and industry in surrounding areas.

In Scandinavia similar schemes are developing. At Malmo (Sweden) the city and county library has compiled a union catalog of technical literature held by industrial firms in the area. The Deichmanske Bibliotek in Oslo is cooperating with local industrial and research libraries to produce a selective union catalog. The Norwegian Technical University Library at Trondheim regularly sends classified accession lists to all major public libraries in the area.

178. Great Britain. Working Party on Inter-library Cooperation in England and Wales. *Inter-library Cooperation in England and Wales: Report of the Working Party Appointed by the Minister of Education in March 1961.* London: H.M.S.O., 1962. 33p.

A committee was appointed to study the technical implications of the recommendation of the Roberts Report in the field of cooperation. The committee calls for a reduction in the number of regional bureaus and statutory responsibility for public library authorities in providing an efficient system of library cooperation in their regions. Other recommendations call for the continuation and improvement of subject specialization and for the completion and simplification of the regional catalogs.

1962

179. Smith, Hannis S. *Cooperative Approach to Library Service.* (American Library Assn. Small Libraries Project Pamphlet, no.16) Chicago: American Library Assn., 1962. 12p.

Smith discusses the advantages of cooperation and outlines some of the areas where cooperation is possible. A specific example of interlibrary cooperation is Minnesota's coordinated system of interlibrary lending involving the Minnesota State Library, Minneapolis and St. Paul Public Libraries, and the University of Minnesota.

180. Horsley, Lucile. "Library Cooperation on the Eastern Shore," *Maryland Libraries* 28: 10-11, 29-31 (Winter 1962).

The Salisbury State Teacher's College in Wicomico County (Md.) has offered the use of its new college library basement to the Wicomico County Libraries. This facility will be used to house the materials for their developing county library system. The space is made available to the libraries and the system rent free and utilities furnished.

181. Bryon, J. F. W. "Beyond Local Boundaries," *Library Journal* 87: 178-81 (15 Jan. 1962).

In 1959, Britain began an interregional scheme of cooperative book purchase, whereby each region accepted responsibility for one section of the Dewey Decimal Classification, excluding fiction. The basis of the scheme is the *British National Bibliography;* wherever a book is classed therein, the appropriate region accepts responsibility for acquisition and permanent storage. There has been insufficient experience, to this date, to determine the acceptability of this approach to cooperation over other broader schemes.

182. "Michigan Goes All Out for Interlibrary Cooperation," *Library Journal* 87: 278-79 (15 Jan. 1962).

The Michigan Joint Committee for School Library Development of the Michigan Association of School Librarians made a series of proposals for improving public and school library relations. One of the proposals made was that joint meetings be held with the Michigan Library Association, the Michigan Association of School Librarians, and the Michigan Education Association along with the Michigan Congress of Parents and Teachers, the Michigan Association of Secondary School Principals, the Michigan Association of School Administrators, the Michigan Audio-Visual Association, the Department of Public Instruction, the Michigan Association of Junior Colleges, the Department of Elementary School Principals, the Michigan unit of the Catholic Library Association, and the Michigan Association of Supervision and Curriculum Development.

183. Fancher, Pauline, and Fancher, Genevieve. "The Creative Elementary School Library and the Public Library," *Wilson Library Bulletin* 36: 555-57 (March 1962).

Cooperation between the public library and the schools in Jamestown (N.Y.) is described. The public library lends books to the schools and offers its facilities for library visits. Cooperative endeavors are planned by the school library consultant, the assistant consultant for elementary school libraries, the public library director, and the children's librarian. The public librarian often teaches library classes in the parochial schools where there is no librarian. In turn, library registration cards are distributed in the schools and annotated booklists for each grade are prepared by the school staffs and kept in the public library.

184. Moore, Helen-Jean. "Library Cooperation in an Urban Setting: The Pittsburgh Story," *Library Trends* 10: 552-61 (April 1962).

In 1948 mutual use of facilities and materials was established by Carnegie Institute of Technology, the University of Pittsburgh, Duquesne University, Chatham College, and Mount Mercy College. Local interlibrary loan services were liberalized and large numbers of loans were made to business and industrial libraries in Pittsburgh. Fifty-six libraries in the Pittsburgh area report serial holdings to a union catalog housed in the Carnegie Library of Pittsburgh. There was also a division of responsibility for special items. Further cooperation is suggested by the author.

185. Reynolds, Michael M. "An Experiment in Regionalism: The Consideration of Research Library Activities in the West Virginia Region," *West Virginia Libraries* 15: 3-7 (June 1962).

West Virginia is proposing a three-year study to determine if a system of regional coordination can be achieved through voluntary cooperation of academic and industrial libraries. A self-supporting system is the aim of the study.

The study hopes to develop the concept of the West Virginia University as a "backstop" collection as well as a bibliographic center for scientific and technical literature searches. Service would be extended to industry and business as well as to other academic institutions and would include storage of materials and the preparation of bibliographies.

Some specific aims of the study would be the development of a book catalog of the scientific, technical, and social science journals of the university and the investigation of the use of graduate assistants for conducting bibliographic searches.

186. Culbertson, Kay. "The Public and College Libraries—Cooperative Services," *Kentucky Library Association Bulletin* 26: 12-18 (July 1962).

One of the more common methods of local cooperation is the exchange of information about holdings and acquisitions. The Philadelphia Union Library Catalog, the union catalog located at the Enoch Pratt Free Library of art books in four Baltimore libraries, and the exchange of information on holdings between the Minnesota Historical Society and the Archives Division of the University of Minnesota Library are examples of exchanging information. Microform projects have encouraged cooperative acquisition programs involving Washington University and the St. Louis Public Library, Wayne State University and the Detroit Public Library, and the University of Utah and the Salt Lake City Public Library. Agreements to divide areas of acquisition have proved difficult to establish and consequently there are few relationships of this type. There has been constructive action in the disposal and exchange of unwanted and duplicate material. Interlibrary loan among local libraries and help for industrial and professional organizations are further areas of cooperation discussed here.

187. Gardner, Frank M. "Cooperation between Research and Public Libraries in Great Britain," *Canadian Library Association Feliciter* 8: 7-17 (Sept. 1962).

Gardner covers the history, present status, and future prospects of cooperation between research and public libraries in Great Britain. Interlibrary loans, union lists, and photocopy service are specific features covered. Organizations such as the Sheffield Interchange Organization (SINTO), Cooperative Industrial and Commercial Reference and Information Service (CICRIS), and the Tyneside Association of Libraries for Industry and Commerce (TALIC) are given as specific examples of such cooperative activity. A bibliography of items describing these and other cooperative activities is included.

188. Poindron, P. "Relations in France between Specialized and Research Libraries and Public Libraries," *Canadian Library Association Feliciter* 8: 5-6 (Sept. 1962).

The importance of municipal libraries for the universities in France is interestingly pointed out here. Municipal libraries contain material from libraries confiscated during the Revolution, and therefore contain important printed matter prior to the nineteenth century. The plan of cooperative acquisitions between the two types of libraries is also described.

189. Malek, Rudolf. "Cooperation between People's Libraries and Research Libraries in Czechoslovakia," *Canadian Library Association Feliciter* 8: 3-13 (Oct. 1962).

Cooperation between libraries in Czechoslovakia began after World War II; during that war 4,000 public libraries were destroyed. The Unified Library System Act of 1959 provides for cooperation between libraries. "Every library is obliged to lend any book or series of books to any library asking for its loan. Consideration must also be given to coordinating the purchase of literature, book exchange, information service, routine methods, book imports from abroad and book publicity."

190. Heintze, Ingeborg. "Cooperation between Research Libraries and Public Libraries in Sweden, *"Libri* 12: 273-82 (no.3). This article appears also in *Canadian Library Association Feliciter* 8: 3-10 (Nov. 1962).

The general organization of Swedish libraries is discussed first, followed by a thorough description of Sweden's extensive system of interlibrary lending between different types of libraries. Other cooperative activities include union catalogs of periodicals of different types of libraries, and joint committees of research and public libraries for consideration of common problems. A revised and enlarged edition of the Swedish classification scheme was the result of the work of the joint Classification and Catalog Committee.

1963

191. Humphry, John A., and Wickersham, Lucille. *Library Cooperation: The Brown University Study of University-School-Community Library Coordination in the State of Rhode Island.* Providence: Brown Univ. Pr., 1963. 213p.

The Council on Library Resources provided a $24,000 grant to study "means of more effectively coordinating state, university, community, and school library service." Following sections on historical background and present status, recommendations are made to achieve improved coordination of library resources and services. Public library systems are advocated, complete with regional resource centers and central libraries, and special responsibilities are assigned to Brown University, the University of Rhode Island, and Rhode Island College. Library councils are suggested as a means of bringing coordination of community and public school services to children and young people. Such councils are to have representatives from the school systems, library trustees, city or town officers, library staffs, interested laymen, and students from public and private schools. Such councils should work on the premise that "schools provide the instructional materials, and county libraries provide supplementary and enriching materials."

192. White, Ruth M. *The School-Housed Public Library—A Survey.* (Public Library Reporter, no.11) Chicago: American Library Assn., 1963. 62p.

Questionnaires were sent to 70 public libraries with branches in public schools and to 84 main public libraries located in schools. The study attempts in a very general way to compare the level of service given in school-housed branches and in independently housed branches. A summary of replies to the questionnaire is given, but no recommendations are made.

Problems related to location, purpose, administration, staff, duplication in book collections, economy, and other areas are considered. Minimum requirements for locating a public library branch in a school are discussed.

School-housed branches and independently housed branches are compared by completeness of reference service, circulation, adult-centered programs, participation in community activities, hours of service, professional staff, and responsibility to the community. School-housed branches fell below independently housed branches in these areas due primarily to restricted size and the requirements of the school.

Specific experiences in eight situations are reported as are statements for and against the arrangement.

193. Dennis, Willard K. "New Library for Buffalo," *School and Community* 49: 12-13 (Jan. 1963).

The Southwest Regional Library of Missouri and the Buffalo (Mo.) High School cooperate to provide library service to both the public and school children by housing a branch library on the school campus. Advantages and disadvantages are enumerated.

194. Burr, Elizabeth. "Study on Public Library-School Relationships Questionnaire," *Wisconsin Library Bulletin* 59: 120-25 (March-April 1963).

A questionnaire was sent to public libraries in Wisconsin on the relationships between the public library and the schools. Some of the conclusions were that public librarians were attending institutes or workshops devoted to cooperation between school and public librarians; and there seemed to be a good deal of communication between public library staffs and school librarians, teachers, and administrators. Although there was communication, not many definite policies had been adopted by library boards. There were deposits of classroom collections in elementary schools, but fewer of these collections were provided for junior and senior high schools.

195. Klitzke, Lewis W. "Public and School Libraries Cooperate," *Illinois Libraries* 45: 217-19 (April 1963).

Klitzke details some of the problems the Des Plaines (Ill.) Public Library faced in meeting the demands of high school students and reports on a survey of use of the public library by students in one of the city's high schools. Meetings between the public library and the high schools resulted in extension of school library hours where this was possible, strengthening of the school libraries' reference collections, and sending of notice to the public library in advance of special assignments.

196. Richardson, Harold G. "The Proposed Houston Technical Information Center," *Special Libraries* 54: 297-99 (May 1963).

Rapid increases in population and industrial expansion and resulting information needs led public, academic, and special librarians of Houston to establish a Committee for the Development of Library Resources. The committee drew up plans for a Technical Information Center which would provide access to the information sources of Houston and the country. The center is to be a nonprofit, research, and industry-oriented organization, supported on a fee basis, and will further cooperation among the 50 libraries of the area.

Other activities of the committee include production of the *Houston List* of scientific and technological serials. Services which the center hopes to provide are rapid interlibrary loan service, inexpensive reproduction, research service, and depository functions for government reports.

197. Van Riemsdijk, G. A. "Cooperation between Research Libraries and Public Libraries in the Netherlands," *Canadian Library Association Feliciter* 8: 3-8 (May 1963).

The inadequacy of public libraries in the Netherlands has led to increased pressure on the university and research libraries to supply materials and services which the public libraries should be providing. Some of the solutions being considered are specialization in six or seven of the largest public libraries, the organization of smaller libraries around one of the larger ones, with university and research libraries being called on for materials the public libraries cannot provide. Union catalogs and rapid communications are other requirements under consideration.

198. Galloway, R. Dean. "Cooperative Acquisitions for California's Libraries," *California Librarian* 24: 183-87 (July 1963).

Galloway points out the need for cooperative acquisitions in California and outlines the essentials for a master plan. A review of efforts and accomplishments to date is presented.

199. "Library Cooperation in Connecticut," *Wilson Library Bulletin* 38: 125 (Oct. 1963).

A cooperative organization called the Library Group of Southwestern Connecticut has been formed that includes 15 laboratories and research firms, public libraries, and the University of Connecticut. The Ferguson Library in Stamford, Connecticut, has compiled a directory of library resources in the Stamford area and a union list of scientific periodicals in local research organizations.

200. Otternik, Gosta. "Swedish Library Cooperation," *Library Journal* 88: 4316-18 (15 Nov. 1963).

Several aspects of cooperation in Sweden and some of the conditions which facilitate it are discussed. Interlibrary loan service is widely used and is helped by the fact that the university libraries are exempted from postal fees. Centralized cataloging can be done on a wide scale because these are common cataloging rules and a uniform classification system. Various Swedish library associations play an important role in cooperation which extends to the other Scandinavian countries. A common Scandinavian library congress every fourth year is one example.

201. Merritt, Bernice. "Students and the Library—in Darien," *CLA News and Views* 5: 6 (Dec. 1963).

Schools and the public library in Darien (Conn.) cooperate in several ways. Teachers were asked to survey resources before making assignments and to inform the public library of these assignments. New teachers are given a tour of the public library at the beginning of the school year and are asked to survey resources of their subjects. Meetings of departments of the junior and senior high schools are held at the public library. "To protect the student who has searched the public library in vain for suitable material on an assigned subject, slips were designed to be signed by responsible reference workers and returned to teachers. Duplicates of these slips will be kept to determine materials that do not exist at the appropriate level, or that are needed as acquisitions either by the school or public libraries."

202. O'Keefe, Richard L. "Relationships of the University Library to Industry and to other Libraries," *SLA Texas Chapter Bulletin* 14: 19-24 (no.4, 1963).

The story of Rice University's service to industry and other libraries in the Houston area is detailed here. This cooperation includes the *Houston List of Scientific and Technical Serial Publications.*

1964

203. *A Joint College/Industry Library with Automata.* Prepared for Harvey Mudd College, Science and Engineering, Claremont, Calif. Reprinted by the Council on Library Resources, Inc. Washington, D.C.: 1964. 35p.

Findings of a study to determine how a machine system for information storage and retrieval can facilitate a cooperative regional library serving a college and industry are reported here. The needs of the Claremont Colleges and area industry for library holdings and services in the physical sciences, mathematics, and engineering were studied to see if such a cooperative venture would be practicable. Results include a list of desired periodical holdings, a definition of the need for bibliographic searching, a preliminary design of an automated system to assist in searching, and estimated costs. Desired holdings total about 1,100 titles representing 70,000 entries annually. Bibliographic searching includes being able to give a requester 24-hour service on all articles appearing on a subject in the last five years. The report concludes that a man-machine system can be established with available hardware. The cost of the system would be shared by the college and industry.

204. Bodker, Adele, and Anzalone, Virginia. "Working Together: Public, School and College Libraries Cooperate in Tangipahoa Parish," *LLA Bulletin* 27: 175-76 (Winter 1964).

The history of cooperation by the schools of Tangipahoa Parish, especially the Center for Materials of Instruction, the Public Library, and Southeastern College, Hammond (La.), is detailed here.

205. Haas, Warren J. "Statewide and Regional Reference Service," *Library Trends* 12: 405-12 (Jan. 1964).

Haas points out the major characteristics of reference networks and describes some which are in operation. Those involving different types of libraries are New York State's 3-R Program and the Pennsylvania Plan. Most of the others involve public and state libraries. A bibliography lists other descriptive articles.

206. Humphry, John A. "Effective Relations Between Libraries: The Massachusetts and Rhode Island Plans," *Texas Library Journal* 40: 51-55 (Summer 1964).

The Western Regional Public Library System of western Massachusetts has one of its members, Forbes Library in Northampton, maintain a membership in the Hampshire Inter-Library Center which is supported by the University of Massachusetts, Smith, Mount Holyoke, and Amherst Colleges. The article is mostly about the development of library systems in the two states and proposed cooperation.

207. Downs, Robert B. "Library Cooperation in Kansas City," *College and Research Libraries* 25: 380-84 (Sept. 1964).

The Kansas City Regional Council for Higher Education was established in 1962 to encourage and promote cooperative planning in and near Kansas City. Downs gives recommendations for (1) developing Kansas City Public Library and Linda Hall Library as bibliographical centers for the region; (2) transferring materials from academic libraries to Kansas City Public and Linda Hall Libraries for storage; and (3) completing the regional union list of serials now in progress.

208. Pooler, Jack, and Weber, David C. "The Technical Information Service in the Stanford University Libraries," *College and Research Libraries* 25: 393-99 (Sept. 1964).

In 1958 Stanford University established a separate library department, the Technical Information Service (TIS), to handle requests from business and industry in the Palo Alto area. In order to use TIS, a firm or industry must be within 50 miles of Stanford. Fees for information service are based on a number of factors. Reading room use; loans of materials by telephone, mail, or in person; reference service; interlibrary loans from libraries other than Stanford; and a voice in the acquisition of library material are some of the services a company may receive. Furnishing specific items by loan or photocopy has been the service most used. TIS has also cooperated in the compilation of the *Union List of Serials Currently Received in the Science Libraries at Stanford.* TIS members may purchase the list at $15 per copy.

209. "Summary Reports: Programs Under the Public Library Development Act of 1963," *News Notes of California Libraries* 59: 430-88 (Fall 1964).

These are 21 separate reports of activity in planning for improved library service and for library systems in California under the state's Public Library Development Act passed in 1963. Most of the reports deal with preliminary planning surveys and proposed programs. While some mention the eventual possibility of incorporating all types of libraries in the programs, the emphasis is on public libraries working together.

1965

210. Blasingame, Ralph. *Library Service in West Virginia; Present and Proposed.* Charleston, W.V.: Library Commission, 1965. 165p.

The existing library service of West Virginia is reviewed and analyzed in relation to educational, socioeconomic, and topographic characteristics of the state. The objective of the study was to develop a meaningful plan for library development. One of the recommendations was the "development of state reference resources and a communication network to facilitate the rapid flow of information between institutions and between institutions and persons." Cooperation of government, people, and all types of libraries was indicated as necessary for obtaining funds and materials to provide easy access to useful library material.

211. Nelson Associates, Inc. *Suggested Guidelines for a Comprehensive Survey of Reference and Research Library Cooperation in Michigan.* New York: Nelson Associates, Inc., 1965. 20p.

The aim of this report was to set forth guidelines which could be constructively employed in the planning of a comprehensive survey of reference and research library resources throughout the state of Michigan. A good deal of cooperation already exists: there is a Union List of Periodicals for the Kalamazoo Area (13 cooperating libraries); Wayne State University maintains a union list of biomedical series for the Detroit area (35 cooperating libraries); Wayne State University Library is preparing a union list of newspapers of metropolitan Detroit; and the Detroit Public Library has a union card catalog incorporating the holdings of the Detroit Institute of Arts.

212. Whittier (Calif.) Area Library Study Committee. *Public Library-School Library Study.* Whittier, Calif.: Office of the Los Angeles County Supt. of Schools, 1965. 116p.

This study explores ways to meet the library needs of a student population in the Whittier area. A committee was formed to study the problem of library use and a set of questionnaires was designed "to secure a sampling of opinion from students and adults to determine what the people felt were their most serious needs with respect to library services and materials, and in what areas there seemed to be the greatest shortages." The answers to the questionnaires revealed "a strong plea for more library books, more librarians, and more library space." It would seem that more cooperative effort will be needed on the part of school libraries and public libraries. One suggestion coming out of the study seemed novel: "Plans are being made for a representative group of students to develop a behavior code or self-governing plan which it is hoped their fellow students will follow."

213. "Nassau Studies Public-School Library Cooperation," *NYLA Bulletin* 13: 9-10 (Jan. 1965).

Mrs. Dinah Lindauer, with a $20,000 federal grant, is studying, under the Nassau Library System, library-school relations to find new ways that public libraries can supplement and complement school libraries.

214. Stevens, Janet R. T. "Pratt's Service to Students," *Wilson Library Bulletin* 39: 384-88 (Jan. 1965).

The article describes a pilot program conducted by the Enoch Pratt Free Library involving the creation of the position of school liaison librarian. The objectives of the program are stated, and the activities of this librarian in coordinating the work of teachers, school librarians, and public library staff are described. The project resulted in the creation of a permanent position of liaison librarian.

215. Byington, Janice J. "Cooperation in This Age of Change," *North Country Libraries* 8: 5-8 (Jan.-Feb. 1965).

The Free Public Library Service in Montpelier has a union file of the holdings of all the public libraries in Vermont. Many examples are given of public library-school cooperation in Vermont.

216. Daane, Beth. "Pulling Together," *Florida Libraries* 16: 23-24, 56-57 (June 1965).

Librarians from the Gainesville (Fla.) Public Library, school librarians from the junior and senior high schools of Gainesville, and reference and circulation librarians from the University of Florida have been meeting to find ways to help students in obtaining materials for class assignments. It was agreed that teachers should give advance notice of large assignments to school librarians, and that school librarians should forward this information to the public library. An agreement was reached that students should use the university library as a last resort. Another cooperative venture between the public library and school librarians involved attempts to prepare preschool children for reading by story-telling programs and by providing easier access to books.

217. McIntyre, John P. "Service to Students—A Joint Responsibility of School and Public Libraries: Library Cooperation in Dade County," *ALA Bulletin* 59: 540-42 (June 1965).

Miami libraries, public and school, have a "working-together spirit" to provide the richest reading experiences possible to the youth of that area. Reciprocal visits and joint exhibits, projects, and career days are designed to develop the habit of using the libraries' resources.

218. Stevens, Frank A. "Public and School Librarians: Partners in Education," *Bookmark* 24: 261-63 (June 1965).

Stevens enumerates some of the problems involved in public and school librarianship, and then goes on to mention some local cooperative programs that have been attempted in the New York City area. Some of these programs are: "establishing a reserve shelf for student assignments at the local public library" and "using paperback books in school and public libraries for duplication of key titles and stimulation of reading."

219. McClaskey, Harris C. "Standard Library Service for Washington's Institutions," *Pacific Northwest Library Association Quarterly* 29: 251-52 (July 1965).

In July 1965, a program was started for "standard library service for Washington's institutions." The aim of the program is to give better library service to such institutions as hospitals, correctional institutions, and schools for the retarded. The program hopes to give a higher level of service at lower cost through cooperative arrangements between public libraries and the various state institutions.

220. Tucker, Harold W., and Hennessy, Mildred L. "The Queens Borough Public Library at Work with Its Schools," *ALA Bulletin* 59: 649-52 (July-Aug. 1965).

The Queens Borough Public Library's program to meet increasing student demands on the public library is described. Efforts have been concentrated on communication with public and parochial schools in an effort to make the schools aware of what problems exist and to work cooperatively for their solution.

221. Wezeman, Frederick. *Combination School and Public Libraries in Pennsylvania; A Study with Recommendations.* Harrisburg, Pa.: The Pennsylvania State Library, Aug. 1965. 35p. (Additional appendix material in some copies)

A survey of 25 school-public "combination" libraries in Pennsylvania was made to determine whether, and under what conditions, state aid should be given to such libraries.

The author reviews some of the literature and relates Michigan's experiences with such libraries. He concludes that such "combination" libraries result in inadequate and substandard public library service and recommends a move toward the establishment of separate public libraries.

222. Frankenfeld, Mrs. Herbert. "Avenues of Cooperation," *ALA Bulletin* 59: 744-45 (Sept. 1965).

The development of communication between the Norristown (Pa.) Public Library, which is a district center library, with school libraries in the area is described. Cooperative activities include assignment notifications, rotating displays, duplicate exchanges, classroom collections, and channels for communication and publicity.

223. Yungmeyer, Elinor. "Cooperation in Action," *ALA Bulletin* 59: 733-44 (Sept. 1965).

This article reports on responses to a memorandum in the *ALA Bulletin* for information on successful school-public library activities in the United States and abroad. Some of the activities reported are: joint book review meetings, preparation of a video tape showing the uses of the library, orientation talks to school children, book fairs, reading programs, workshops on common problems, joint planning for total library development, advance assignment notification, preparation of descriptive handbooks, cooperative supervision of students in the public library, and several others. About 15 states are represented in the responses.

224. Martin, Gene. "Interlibrary Cooperation in Missouri," *Wilson Library Bulletin* 40: 166-71 (Oct. 1965).

Missouri Library Service: A Guide to Its Development and Standards of Service, which was officially adopted in October 1963, is discussed in this article. The objective of the *Guide* was "the achievement of a statewide network of library service, with every library in the state being a part of a library system, each separate system relating in turn to other systems until the network is complete." Library systems were to include all types of libraries—public, school, college, university, and special.

225. "Better Service to Students," *Bookmark* 25: 116 (Dec. 1965).

Many steps were being taken in 1965 in New York State to provide more cooperation between public librarians, school librarians, and teachers. Westchester Library System has published *Patterns of Partnership* which suggests ways in which teachers can work with public libraries.

1966

226. Bonn, George S. *Science-Technology Literature Resources in Canada; Report of a Survey for the Associate Committee on Scientific Information.* Ottawa, Canada: National Research Council, 1966. 80p.

This survey of Canadian university, provincial research council, and major public libraries was designed to assess strengths and weaknesses in science-technology holdings.

Bonn recommends that the National Research Council Library be made the National Science Library of Canada and proposes the creation of a "Science Service Library" network under the direction of the National Science Library. The network would consist of publicly supported libraries and would attempt to provide service to all populated areas. Responsibility for service in an area would be assigned to a public library which in turn would be compensated for giving the service. Grants to strengthen book collections would be made, and all libraries would be tied by teletype to the National Science Library.

Further details of operation are provided together with a rationale for the program.

227. Jefferson, George. *Library Cooperation.* New York: London House & Maxwell, 1966. 160p.

Jefferson's work is a comprehensive coverage of library cooperation in Great Britain and includes a bibliography. The growing number of special libraries, the post-war expansion of educational facilities, and the "professionalization of librarianship" all led to the idea of cooperation as a responsibility and an extension of library service and as a means of providing an integrated national library service. There are chapters on cooperative storage and acquisitions, scientific and technical literature, tools of cooperation, international cooperation, and the future of cooperation in Britain.

228. Silvester, Elizabeth et al. *Some Aspects of Library Cooperation in the Province of Quebec: A Report of the Inter-Library Cooperation Committee of the University and College Libraries Section.* (Publication no.6) Montreal: Quebec Library Assn., 1966. 12p.

Using a two-part questionnaire, a survey was made of a sample of all types of libraries in Quebec to determine what services libraries extended to users other than their regular registered borrowers, and what policies governed interlibrary loans. Questionnaires were sent to 188 libraries and 112 replies were received. The major conclusions of the survey were that cooperation between libraries in Quebec is "quite haphazard and unplanned" and formalization and standardization of practices and policies are necessary.

229. Wallis, C. Lamar. "Tennessee Reference Centers," *Southeastern Librarian* 16: 226-30 (Winter 1966).

Four public libraries in Tennessee (Nashville, Knoxville, Chattanooga, and Memphis) serve as reference centers for surrounding areas. The University of Tennessee and the TVA library also furnish information as needed. The centers accept requests from libraries, business and industry, and regional library centers. Information is provided by direct telephone answers, photoduplication of materials, and interlibrary loans. The program is funded by LSCA. A supporting aid to the Memphis center is the *Union List of Serials in the Memphis Area* compiled by the Memphis Librarians' Committee, a group comprised of school, college and university, public, and special librarians.

230. McJenkins, Virginia. "Library Service to Secondary School Students; Its Problems and Opportunities for Schools and Public Libraries," *National Association of Secondary School Principals Bulletin* 50: 10-17 (Jan. 1966).

This article places great stress on the role of the school principal in creating quality school libraries. Having school libraries open in the evenings, on Saturdays, and holidays is suggested for relieving the pressure on public libraries. The Montclair School and Public Library Relations Committee (SPLARC) in New Jersey is mentioned as an example of good communication between public and school libraries.

231. Taylor, Frank R. "Library Service to Industry in Great Britain and on the Continent," *Library Trends* 14: 306-31 (Jan. 1966).

Taylor gives an historical survey of the development of service to industry by libraries in Great Britain. Service by public libraries, including the establishment of separate technical libraries, service by technical colleges and county authorities, and the establishment of cooperative arrangements are described. Among the cooperative efforts described are the Sheffield Interchange Organization (SINTO), Manchester Technical Information Service (MANTIS), Cooperative Industrial Commercial Reference and Information Service (CICRIS), Hull Technical Interloan Scheme (HULTIS), Liverpool and District Scientific Industrial and Research Library Advisory Council (LADSIRLAC), Tyneside Association of Libraries for Industry and Commerce (TALIC), Huddersfield and District Information Scheme (HADIS), Northeast Lancashire Technical Advisory Service (NELTAS), and several others.

Consideration is also given to efforts to develop these regional groups into a plan for cooperation on a national basis. The discussion of cooperative efforts on the continent is fairly brief and reports that except for Germany and Holland few exist.

232. Winkler, Loretta M. "Cooperation and Coexistence: Public and School Libraries," *Top of the News* 22: 188-93 (Jan. 1966).

This is a report of Westchester County's (N.Y.) effort to improve the county's public library service to high school students. The author served as public library-school relations consultant in charge of the one-year project.

Phase one of the program was aimed at improving communications and included visits to schools to obtain lists of needed materials and to offer assistance in providing materials. A leaflet, *Pattern for Partnership,* offered ideas for cooperation and served also as the basis for joint discussions.

Phase two of the project was concerned with providing needed materials, and phase three consisted of a questionnaire to junior and senior high school students to determine the dimensions of the need for materials. A final step was a questionnaire to young adults on what their needs were in the public library.

Considerable success was reported in opening up channels of communication; other phases of the program were still in evaluation stages.

233. Woods, Bill M. "Regional and National Co-ordination and Planning," *Library Trends* 14: 295-305 (Jan. 1966).

Most of the cooperative activities discussed here involve special libraries working together in various ways, but mention is made of projects which include cooperation with other types of libraries. Among the latter are Houston's Regional Information and Communication Exchange (RICE), the Library Group of Southwestern Connecticut, and several projects in California involving both university and special libraries. The potential role of the special library in the developing reference and research networks is also discussed.

234. Curley, Walter W. "Project: A School Library System for All Public and Private Schools in the County, to Pool Resources, Provide Bibliographic Control through a Union Catalog, and Provide Centralized Services Ranging from Selection to Delivery; Patterned on a Public Library Cooperative System." (Sample Projects, Title III, ESEA), *Library Journal* 91: 1029-31, 56 (15 Feb. 1966).

Curley describes a Title III proposal to create a library system for public and private school libraries of Suffolk County, Long Island. The proposal of the Suffolk Cooperative Library System was to extend its services to school libraries. The services of the system "would include selection, purchase, processing, distribution on loan and delivery of a massive collection of books and audio-visual materials that supplement local library resources, along with equipment for their use." An abstract from the project application is included.

235. Lindauer, Dinah S. "Project: Approved by the U.S. Office of Education. To Inventory Resources, Study Existing Services and Set Up Pilots, Toward the Creation of an Interlocking System of Regional Services, Including a Library Phase" (Sample Projects, Title III, ESEA), *Library Journal* 91: 1025-28 (15 Feb. 1966).

Under Title III of ESEA the Nassau (N.Y.) Library System set up a public library-school liaison project. One of the purposes of the project was to "explore the feasibility of contracting with school libraries in the county for selected services now provided by the Nassau Library System only to its member public libraries." In Nassau County there are more than 400,000 school-age children that are educated in "400 public and private school buildings in 56 independent school districts, each administered by its own board of education. . . . There are no agencies at the county level to enable this plethora of school districts to coordinate policies, share materials or facilities, or plan cooperatively to meet the mushrooming complexity and costs of education."

236. Drake, Christine. "Public Libraries Find Needed Information Through University Extension Services," *Mississippi Library News* 30: 28, 38 (March 1966).

This article deals with four services to public libraries from the University of Mississippi's extension department. The Drama Loan Library lends plays for reading purposes only, for a period of three weeks on payment of postal costs. Materials on the high school debate topic are distributed to schools either free or for a minimal charge. A third service, the Program Package Service, distributes materials on topical, cultural, or educational subjects for the use of program planners. A final service supplies books to public libraries for the use of patrons participating in Home Reading Courses of Mississippi's Federation of Women's Clubs.

237. Blackshear, Orrilla T., and Taylor, Kenneth I. "School-Public Library Cooperation, Madison," *Wisconsin Library Bulletin* 62: 97, 99 (March-April 1966).

Cooperation between Madison Public Library and the city's public schools takes many forms. An exchange program was inaugurated in which a public librarian spent a week at a senior high school library and vice versa. In 1966 a brochure was planned to explain school and public library service. A study was begun "to determine which collections and services should be duplicated and which should remain supplementary."

238. Little, Robert, and Kaczmarek, Carol. "School-Public Library Cooperation, Door County," *Wisconsin Library Bulletin* 62: 94-96 (March-April 1966).

The public and school librarians of Door County (Wis.) have participated in a number of cooperative projects for meeting the needs of students. The public and school librarians met and decided that certain units of study would be taught at different times in different schools to avoid runs on resources. At joint meetings of the librarians displays of new books are provided for examination and book selection is discussed so that each librarian learns what the other libraries are purchasing. A union catalog of magazines was compiled and each library received a set of the cards. Joint ordering and processing of books was started in the belief that this would enable the school librarian to spend more time working with students. An increased interloan of materials was noted by all the librarians. A joint film library is also maintained.

239. Winkler, Loretta M., and Losinski, Julia. "An Epilogue: Cooperation and Coexistence," *Top of the News* 22: 323-26 (April 1966).

The Westchester Library System's paperback experiment and the student survey on books and library service are described. Paperbacks of known popularity among students were placed in six member libraries of the system. A complete circulation count for each title was kept over a seven month period, and the experiment was considered a success. A 20-item questionnaire on library service to young adults was filled out by 2,000 students. One of the findings was that students use public libraries for both school required reading and for reading for their own interests.

240. "Shared Cataloging Arrangement with British National Bibliography," *Library of Congress Information Bulletin* 25: 238-39 (12 May 1966).

During April 1966, the Library of Congress printed and distributed the first catalog cards prepared under an experimental cooperative arrangement with the British National Bibliography. LC receives copies of BNB cards three weeks in advance of publication of the *Bibliography*. Reduction in duplication of effort is seen as the chief advantage, and should prove important as a first step toward international cooperation in cataloging.

241. Leonard, Virginia. "Book Selection in Grosse Pointe: Where School Librarians Advise the Public Library," *ALA Bulletin* 60: 627-29 (June 1966).

The book selection committee of the Grosse Point (Mich.) Public Library —consisting of the chief of the Central Library, the chief of children's services, the two branch librarians, the heads of the circulation and processing departments, and the director—invited representatives of all public, private, and parochial schools to attend its meetings. The format of a typical meeting is described along with a list of reviewing media used in book selection. The objective is general improvement in library service to students.

242. Swank, R. C. "Survey of the Bibliographical Center for Research." *Mountain-Plains Library Quarterly* 11: 3-6 (Fall 1966).

Following a survey of the Bibliographic Center for Research—Rocky Mountain Region, Swank recommended that:

- A consistent state by state pattern of full reporting to the Bibliographical Center of acquisitions by the major university and public libraries and by the state be established
- A conference of representatives of public, academic, school, and special libraries from each of the states of the region be convened by the center to study the potentials of a regional network of state library reference systems embracing all types of libraries, with the Bibliographical Center serving as the coordinating agency
- An ad hoc committee study the bibliographic needs of the region as they relate to mechanization; the type of systems that would best serve the purposes of the region, especially those of the public libraries; and the relationships of those systems with the Colorado academic libraries processing center.

1967

243. American Library Association. *Proceedings of the 1967 Midwinter Meeting and the 86th Annual Conference.* Chicago: The Association, n.d. 292p.

Jane T. Thurston describes the formation of the Yakima Valley Regional Library. This region is undertaking a coordinated acquisition policy and a union list of periodicals (p.192).

244. Avins, Wesley, comp. *Union List of Periodicals of Fort Wayne Area Libraries.* Fort Wayne, Ind.: Public Library of Fort Wayne and Allen County, 1967. 148p.

Thirty libraries in the Fort Wayne area contributed to this union list. In addition to the public library, the holdings of a number of industrial, special, and school libraries are included.

245. Blasingame, Ralph. *Feasibility of Cooperation for Exchange of Resources among Academic and Special Libraries in Pennsylvania.* University Park: The Pennsylvania State Univ., 1967. 28p.

The purpose of this study was to examine cooperation between special and academic libraries and to suggest future means of cooperation. Throughout the study there are observations on the possibilities of a cooperative system for the exchange of resources among academic and special libraries. Requirements for such a system are given and "major areas for potential immediate state action" are listed.

246. Edelman, Hendrik. *Shared Acquisitions and Retention System (SHARES) for the New York Metropolitan Area, a Proposal for Cooperation Among METRO Libraries.* (METRO Miscellaneous Publication, no.3) New York: Metropolitan Reference and Research Library Agency, 1967. 21p.

A number of proposals are made: SHARES should develop long range plans with regard to cooperation in acquisitions and possibly cooperative and/or centralized processing. "Another suggestion is that METRO should contract with one or more libraries in its geographical area to take responsibility for the retention of last copies of certain types of materials or of material in defined subject areas." Creation of a separate storage facility is not called for. "After careful study and extensive discussions we have reached the conclusion that the creation of a separate storage facility for METRO would not be desirable at this time. An important argument was the lack of any quantitative data and the lack of firm commitments of librarians, except for short term use of the space." A bibliography is included.

247. Little, Arthur D., Inc. *A Plan for Library Cooperation in New Hampshire. Report to New Hampshire State Library.* Cambridge, Mass.: Arthur D. Little, Inc., 1967. 68p.

This study was conducted as the initial step in New Hampshire's long range program of improvement in its library service. The main objective of the plan is to improve reader service by coordinating the resources of many libraries to make them more fully available and to extend more effective service to institutions and the handicapped.

A series of recommendations under interlibrary cooperation call for improved communications by the compilation of union lists and the installation of telephone and teletype circuits, reproduction equipment, and telefacsimile facilities for the state library.

Other areas of cooperation suggested were the improvement and extension of interlibrary loan service, cooperative strengthening of resources of nonbook materials, institution of a common borrower's card, delivery service, centralized ordering and processing, and cooperative book selection.

Other recommendations dealt with the participation of school, academic, and special libraries and the New Hampshire State Library in a statewide network and with means for the improvement of staff. It was also suggested that the possibility of a New England library network be investigated.

248. Lorenz, John G. "Regional and State Systems," in Winifred B. Linderman, ed., *The Present Status and Future Prospects of Reference/Information Service,* p.73-82. Proceedings of the Conference held at the School of Library Service, Columbia University, 30 March-1 April 1966. Chicago: American Library Assn., 1967.

Lorenz discusses the development of regional and state library systems with emphasis on their role in reference and information service. Most of the examples cited pertain to public libraries, but mention is made of Indiana's Communication System and of New York's Regional Reference and Research Library Program, both of which involve different types of libraries.

In Indiana, the state library, 30 local public libraries, four state university libraries, and three other academic or special libraries are connected by TWX for the purpose of making reference resources more widely available through the state. The network handles reference referrals, interlibrary loans, and other communications. Smaller libraries may contact the nearest member library to take advantage of the system.

The New York program is, as it was in the planning stage, a network of academic, special, and public libraries with various adaptations for different geographic areas.

249. Morchand, Charles A. *Preliminary Study for an Improved Information Transfer System for Metropolitan Libraries.* (METRO Miscellaneous Publication, no.2) New York: Metropolitan Reference and Research Library Agency, 1967. 10p.

The New York Metropolitan Reference and Research Library Agency, Inc. (METRO) is made up of about 50 libraries of different types in the New York City area. This study "has been prepared with the aim of providing an outline for an initial information transfer network within a 50-mile radius of Times Square." The Morchand Transmission (Video) System is discussed as an answer to problems of communication between METRO libraries.

250. Hill, Laurence G., and Goldberg, Dorothy. "Public Library-School Cooperation: LSCA-ESEA, 1964-1966," *Bookmark* 26: 111-12 (Jan. 1967).

In 1964 the Nioga Library System (N.Y.) received LSCA funds for a program to promote school-public library cooperation. A full-time professional librarian was hired by the system "to enlist full cooperation among school librarians, teachers, and public librarians, and to plan and implement means to make the most effective use of library resources, school and public, in the Nioga area." The system also purchased photoreproduction equipment, microfilm readers, microfilm reader-printers, and periodicals on microfilm. This material and equipment was placed "at strategic locations in the system." Nineteen public libraries and 28 school districts were involved in this cooperative project. One point emphasized was "that the approach to cooperation between school and public libraries must be made simultaneously at the administrative and at the teacher-librarian levels." Part of the coordinator's job has been to act "as a clearinghouse for specific problems in mass assignments, term paper research, special topics, location of materials and so on." The Nioga Library System also received a grant in 1966 under Title II of the Elementary and Secondary Education Act in order to purchase books to be used in school libraries.

251. Nott, Julie H., and Wheeler, Marjorie. "Library Service by Contract: A Joint Venture," *College and Research Libraries* 28: 107-9 (March 1967).

A long term contract between Southern Methodist University and the Graduate Research Center of the Southwest provides an answer to the problem of university libraries serving smaller special libraries.

252. Murray, Tom. "Information for Business and Industry," *Wisconsin Library Bulletin* 63: 88 (March-April 1967).

Murray describes the University-Industry Research Program (UIR) of the Information Services Division of the University of Wisconsin. UIR's purpose is to make university library facilities available to industry and to act as a clearinghouse to other information resources. Services include on-site use of materials; quick reference service; location, loan, or reproduction of resources; assistance in procurement of various federal reports; brief literature searches; and publication of a *Union List of Serials and Periodicals* held on various science fields at the Madison campus.

253. "A Reference Roundup," *Library Journal* 92: 1582-85 (15 April 1967).

Connecticut and Rhode Island have a program involving both states in a TWX network to join public and academic libraries "to speed reference service to their respective business communities." Cooperative action plans such as METRO in New York are discussed briefly. Colleges in Pennsylvania give public library service to citizens "when they are the institutions best equipped to do so." Rhode Island and Pennsylvania are pioneering in cooperation between special and public libraries.

254. Josey, E. J. "Community Use of Academic Libraries, a Symposium," *College and Research Libraries* 28: 184-202 (May 1967).

This symposium deals with results of a survey on community use of academic libraries to which 783 academic libraries responded. Items included in the questionnaire pertain to the kinds of privileges granted and to whom, restrictions, where imposed, and the reasons for them, fees, and methods used in retrieving books.

Other questions dealt with loans to public libraries and opinions on the feasibility of a statewide library card. There is also a description of the "Interlibrary Loan by Publisher Plan" in use in southern California. In this arrangement a library agrees to purchase all of a publisher's output and to make the material available on interlibrary loan. Another cooperative project mentioned is the *Union List of Periodicals in Evansville (Ind.) Libraries,* which is published annually by a number of local libraries in Evansville.

255. Smith, Hannis S. "Progress Report on Planning for Interlibrary Cooperation," *Minnesota Libraries* 22: 53-55 (Summer 1967).

Smith reviews briefly some of the steps taken toward cooperation among different types of libraries in Minnesota. He discusses the recommendations of the Academic Section of the Minnesota Library Association for a central serial file and a deposit collection of all items reviewed in *CHOICE* and the recommendation for the creation of a Metropolitan Library Service Agency for Minneapolis and St. Paul, which potentially could include academic and special libraries as well as public libraries.

This progress report lists finally the recommendations of the First Minnesota Assembly on Interlibrary Cooperation, a two-day conference involving librarians from all types of libraries from all parts of the state. One of their recommendations is that a central library service agency be created to perform specific services for member libraries with membership open to all types of libraries and funded by state and federal funds and fees from member libraries. The services desired include an interlibrary communication network, the assembling of all known union lists, the collection and dissemination services recommended by the Minnesota Library Association, the hiring of specialized reference personnel who could also coordinate interlibrary loans, and finally the production of union catalogs in printed form.

256. Wells, A. J. "Centralized Cataloging in Great Britain," *Library Trends* 16: 143-48 (July 1967).

The British National Bibliography, the British Museum, the Libraries of the Universities of Oxford and Cambridge, the Library of Trinity College in Dublin, the National Library of Scotland, and the National Library of Wales have set up an ad hoc committee to work toward a standard cataloging practice for British libraries. It is hoped that such a standard will induce libraries to make changes in their local practices in order to conform to a national standard and thus make cooperative cataloging a more practical proposal in Great Britain.

257. Vamberry, Joseph T. "The New Scope and Content of Cooperative Cataloging for Law Libraries," *Law Library Journal* 60: 244-48 (Aug. 1967).

Under the new international shared cataloging program supported by the federal government, the Library of Congress has accepted the responsibility on the national level to acquire important research materials published anywhere in the world and promptly provide cataloging information on them. The Library of Congress supplies cooperating libraries with a copy of each catalog card printed for current imprints. Cooperating libraries send to Library of Congress copies of their orders for current domestic and foreign acquisitions for which no card is found in the National Union Catalog or in the control file.

258. McClaskey, Harris C. "A Cooperative Library Program," *Minnesota Libraries* 22: 75-77 (Autumn 1967).

McClaskey describes how creative cooperation between librarians and other professions is working to improve service in hospitals and institutions in the state of Washington.

259. Connor, Jean L. "Stages in and Fields for Interlibrary Cooperation," *Bookmark* 27: 13-18 (Oct. 1967).

This address to the American Library Trustee Association at the 1967 ALA Conference deals with the questions of the best approach to cooperation and the areas in which cooperation should be promoted. Most of the examples of cooperative activities are taken from New York State. The use of liaison staff is exemplified by programs in the Nassau, Westchester, and Nioga Library Systems. Contractual arrangements for processing of school materials exist in the Suffolk and Nassau systems. A membership system is typified by New York's nine reference and research systems.

In discussing areas where cooperation would be helpful, New York's interlibrary loan system is mentioned along with its facsimile project. Another area in which New York provides an example is delivery service. In the Albany area a daily delivery service links the State Library, three public library systems, six colleges, and several special libraries.

260. Sheridan, Robert N. "Library Cooperation—A Public Librarian's Viewpoint," *Bookmark* 27: 77-81 (Nov. 1967).

The author gives a number of suggestions for effective cooperation between school and public libraries and tells of programs in effect in Levittown (N.Y.). These projects include assignment notification cards, multiple copies of paperback books for use in student assignments, bookmobile stops at elementary schools, preparation and distribution of bibliographies of school and public library holdings, talks at faculty meetings, preparation of curriculum units, and joint publicity projects.

261. Winnick, Pauline, and Horn, William A. "Liaison Librarian," *American Education* 4: 26-27 (Dec. 1967-Jan. 1968).

This article discusses the problem of school-public library coordination and cites examples where liaison librarians have been used to help solve the problem. New York has a school liaison consultant at the state level. Public library-school relations projects and coordinators have been established in the Nassau, Westchester, and Nioga Library Systems in New York and in Prince George's County Memorial Library in Maryland. Activities under the programs include provision of supplementary materials, coordination of loans, and establishment of communication with teachers and school administrators.

1968

262. Bevis, Dorothy. *An Inventory of Library Services and Resources of the State of Washington.* Olympia, Wash.: Washington State Library, 1968. 385p.

This survey was undertaken in order to update information about the needs of public, academic, and school libraries in the state of Washington. There is some discussion of cooperative efforts, the Spokane area union list of periodicals being a specific example involving different types of libraries.

263. Charlotte, N.C. Public Library of Charlotte and Mecklenburg County. *Annual Report, 1967-68.*

The Mecklenburg Library Association published a computer based union list of periodical holdings in February 1966. The Charlotte Area Library Association is preparing a new edition scheduled for completion in 1969, which will include all significant serial and periodical holdings within 50 miles of Charlotte.

264. *Conference on School-Public Library Relations.* New York City, Feb. 8-9, 1968. Albany: New York State Dept. of Education, Div. of Library Development, 1968. 87p.

While concerned primarily with developments in New York, there is much in the proceedings of this conference that will be of general interest. Most of the presentations deal with planning for cooperation and present rather general treatment of the problems, with the exception of E. J. Josey's address on the New York State Interlibrary Loan pilot project (NYSILL) and the Facsimile Transmission experiment (FACTS).

Although specific examples of cooperation are not always given, the articles are presented within the perspective of New York's well-developed program for library service.

265. Hawaii. Department of Education. Office of Library Services. *6th Annual Report, 1967-1968.*

The Hawaii State Library Centralized Processing Center serves 210 public school libraries, 120 private school libraries, 43 public libraries, and the Hawaii Curriculum Center.

266. Holley, Edward G., and Hendricks, Donald D. *Resources of Texas Libraries.* (Coordinating Board, Texas College and University System, Study Paper, no.3) Austin: Coordinating Board, Texas College and University System, 1968. 123p.

Although primarily concerned with identifying weaknesses and strengths in libraries as they relate to the academic scene, this study briefly treats the public library network and emerging cooperative patterns. Mention is made of the *Texas List of Scientific and Technical Serial Publications,* the Industrial Information Service (IIS), and the Regional Information and Communication Exchange (RICE). IIS, based at Southern Methodist University, and RICE, based at Rice University, are State Technical Services Act projects designed to improve service to local business and industry through provision of bibliographic access to academic library collections, literature searching, and dissemination of information to the regional community.

267. University of Houston. Libraries. *Annual Report for the Year 1967-68.* 41p.

This report describes participation in two new teletype networks—Texas Information Exchange (TIE) and Regional Information and Communications Exchange (RICE).

A revised edition of the *Texas List of Scientific and Technical Serial Publications* appeared in the spring of 1968. It contains over 150,000 locations for serials in science, technology, business, commerce, and industry from about 200 libraries in Texas.

268. Murphy, Virginia B., comp. *Newspaper Resources of District V, Texas Library Association, A Union List.* Houston: Univ. of Houston, 1968. 46p.

Fifty public, university, and special libraries in the Houston area contributed to the compilation of this union list. Holdings are listed geographically by country, state, and city of origin.

269. Nelson Associates, Inc. *Library Service in the Capitol Region of Connecticut, A Study with Recommendations for Future Development.* New York: Nelson Associates, Inc., 1968.

The objectives of this study "were to assess existing library resources, services, and needs in the Capitol Region of Connecticut and to recommend steps to be taken to improve these resources and services." There is some cooperation among libraries in the Capitol Region such as reciprocal borrowing privileges and interlibrary loan, but generally there are few cooperative efforts to provide services. One of the conclusions of the study was that "to provide good reference and research library services in the Capitol Region, it is important to make the resources of the academic and special libraries accessible to supplement the limited resources of the public and school libraries."

270. Shank, Russell. *Regional Access to Scientific and Technical Information; A Program for Action in the New York Metropolitan Area.* (METRO Miscellaneous Publications Series, no.1) New York: Metropolitan Reference and Research Library Agency, Inc., 1968. 113p.

This is a study of physical sciences and engineering library and information facilities and services in the New York area. "An attempt was made to assess the effectiveness of various cooperative devices and information service facilities, including: Guides to local science collections; Union lists of local holdings; Rapid communication and transportation facilities among local libraries; The adequacy of copying services; The availability of translators and abstractors; The possibility of formal agreements for divided responsibility in the acquisition and storage of science materials." The basic objective of the report is "to orient libraries and information services in the New York City region towards a system structure that will enhance full exploitation of literature-based information resources in science and technology for the citizens of this particular region, for the State of New York, and finally for the nation."

271. Tucson Public Library. *Annual Report,* 1967-1968.

Nineteen libraries—public, school, university, special, parochial, and others—have formed the Tucson Area Library Council (Ariz.) to discuss mutual interests and problems and to plan for cooperative activities. A committee is preparing a directory of area resources, and the council is anticipating having Tucson serve as one of four resource centers for the state.

In Tucson, a feasibility study is being made of a combined technical processing center for the Tucson Public Library and one of the city's school districts.

272. Houze, Robert A. "CORAL, San Antonio's Success Story in Library Cooperation," *Texas Library Journal* 44: 151-52, 185-88 (Winter 1968).

The Council of Research and Academic Libraries (CORAL) prepared a guide entitled *San Antonio Area Specialized Library Resources* in 1968. This guide includes basic information about academic and special library resources in the area. A union list of serials is also planned.

273. Laursen, Johs. Lehm. "Public Library Cooperation in Greater Copenhagen," *Scandinavian Public Library Quarterly* 1: 65-80 (no.2, 1968).

The Danish Public Libraries Act of 1965 aims at cooperative book purchase between public libraries in Greater Copenhagen and the research libraries of the area. Possibilities of cooperation in interlibrary loan and cataloging were being explored. The public libraries of Denmark lend sets of books to literary study groups, grammar schools, and training colleges. A set consists of 30 books, and 30 sets, or approximately 6,000 volumes, were available for this type of loan. The collection of sets of fiction is in use only in the Copenhagen area, but the collection of children's literature in foreign languages is available throughout Denmark.

274. Stanford, Edward B. "University Library Undertakes MINITEX Interlibrary Service Project," *Minnesota Libraries* 22: 235-36 (Winter 1968).

In December 1968, the University of Minnesota Library announced the beginning of a two-year pilot project to speed up lending and copying service to certain libraries in Minnesota outside of the Minneapolis-St. Paul metropolitan area. The project is known as MINITEX (Minnesota Interlibrary Teletype Experiment) and will include private college, state college, junior college, university branch campus, and public libraries. "The purpose of MINITEX . . . is to obtain cost, volume, and operational data that will provide a basis for developing recommendations for a more long-range state-wide interlibrary service program." The service will use TWX equipment and will try various delivery arrangements (e.g., United Parcel) for getting materials to the requestors.

275. Fischer, Margaret. "Library Cooperation," *Catholic Library World* 39: 332-37 (Jan. 1968).

This short descriptive introduction to the history of library cooperation includes the history of interlibrary loans; cooperative acquisitions projects, such as the Farmington Plan; storage warehouses and interlibrary centers, e.g., the New England Deposit Library, Center for Research Libraries, Hampshire Inter-Library Center; and bibliographical centers and union catalogs, such as the *National Union Catalog, Union List of Serials, List of Serials in Chicago,* the Pacific Northwest Bibliographical Center, *Union Library Catalogue of the Philadelphia Metropolitan Area,* the Rocky Mountain Bibliographical Center, and the *Union Catalog of Northeastern Pennsylvania.*

276. Orne, Jerrold. "A New Pattern of Service," *North Carolina Libraries* 16: 51-54 (Feb. 1968).

Orne describes some of the proposals for improved library service in North Carolina. North Carolina has been building a union catalog for 20 years. In 1968 it contained about a half million cards from 15 major libraries. The University of North Carolina has also had an extension department for 50 years which performed some functions usually handled by state library agencies.

In the future the state library will record the resources of government agencies and offices in Raleigh; all will be centrally cataloged and entered in the state library's records. Public libraries which have agreements with the state library to build collections in special subject fields for statewide interlibrary loan service will have these collections recorded in catalogs in the state library. In turn the state library will report them to the North Carolina Union Catalog.

The Interlibrary Center at the University of North Carolina represents a bibliographic concentration designed to record and make available every item which may be needed in the state, together with the means of informing potential users of location and availability. Inquiries will be sorted at both the state library and the university and directed to the proper source for handling.

277. Brewer, Margaret. "Patterns of Cooperation Among Public and School Libraries," *Missouri Library Association Quarterly* 29: 51-63 (March 1968).

This is a report of a survey conducted to determine recent activities in school-public library cooperation. Responses were received from more than half of the states and U.S. possessions queried. The responses are grouped and discussed under five categories: "(1) Cooperative programs sponsored by the State Library or State Department of Education; (2) Regional library sponsorship of cooperative programs; (3) City library/school library cooperation; (4) Miscellaneous areas of cooperation; and (5) Examples where cooperation of school library/public library has been discouraged or avoided."

Specific examples of each of the types are given and are too numerous to report here. Some of the trends which the author sees as emerging are: public and school libraries operating as one unit; public libraries acting as acquisition and processing centers for schools; school-public library cooperation in book selection; cooperation in offering instruction in the use of libraries.

The author notes that there is a noticeable lack of initiative in many states in encouraging cooperative school-public library programs.

278. "Separate Kansas City School-Public Library Branch Service Urged," *Show-Me Libraries* 19: 5 (March 1968).

In Kansas City (Mo.), where public libraries are operated by the school board, the librarian has called for the complete separation of school and public libraries. Each type of library would operate with its own budget under the direction of the librarian. The librarian urges that the schools provide school-operated libraries in elementary, junior high, and senior high schools and recommends that the public function of the high school libraries be phased out upon completion of six new public library branches.

279. MacDonald, Mary Jane. "Interlibrary Loan Developments: Illinois," *RQ* 7: 116-21 (Spring 1968).

An address on the patterns of interlibrary loan development in Illinois and some of the problems encountered. Requests are referred from the local level to the system headquarters to one of four research centers in the state. The article discusses the role of the research centers, their arrangements with the library systems, and some of the requirements for a successful interlibrary loan program. The program is still in its early stages and subject to rapid changes.

280. Ness, Charles H. "Interlibrary Loan Developments: Pennsylvania," *RQ* 7: 114-16 (Spring 1968).

Ness describes the procedure for interlibrary loans within Pennsylvania's network of local libraries, 30 district libraries, and four resource centers. The resource centers are to develop research collections in specific subject areas. The Union Catalog of Pennsylvania in Philadelphia lists holdings of 123 Pennsylvania libraries and acts as an unofficial research agency for the resource centers.

The path followed by an interlibrary loan request is from the local level to the district center to the state library and from there to the union catalog by teletype when required. The union catalog has yielded locations for 80 percent of the referrals from the state library. Unlocated items are sent to district centers for possible purchase. Reference questions are sent from the district center to the resource center responsible for the subject area. More than 50 percent of all requests originate from students.

281. "Network Speeds Interlibrary Loans," *Texas Libraries* 30: 43 (Spring 1968).

In March 1968, the Texas State Library initiated a teletype network to bring the resources of many libraries to the readers all over Texas through the state's ten major Resource Centers. Federal assistance has been received through Title III of the Library Services and Construction Act.

282. Pike, Eugene. "Interlibrary Loan Developments: California," *RQ* 7: 111-14 (Spring 1968).

Pike describes the procedures the California State Library follows in handling interlibrary loan requests and the state's union catalog to which 80 libraries contribute. The goal is to establish the state library as a statewide reference and research center in order to take some of the load off academic and research libraries.

283. Shephard, Martha. "Interlibrary Loan Developments: Canada," *RQ* 7: 121-25 (Spring 1968).

Work on a national union catalog for Canada began in 1950 and now contains close to nine million cards representing holdings of 276 libraries of various types, but chiefly the reference collections of the larger public libraries.

The union catalog of the National Library may be reached by telephone, mail, Telex, and by personal visits. An average of 200 requests is received each day, of which about 75 percent are filled. The goal is to send out a reply the same day the request is received. Close collaboration is maintained with the National Science Library for searching of requests. The interlibrary loan code is as generous as possible. The

National Library catalog is searched first and the item sent if available; if the library does not have the item, the union catalog is searched for another location. If the requesting library is located some distance away, reproductions are provided for a charge.

284. "Wayne County (Michigan) Federated Library System," *News Lines* 75: 1 (April 1968).

Ten school districts have contracted with the Wayne County (Mich.) Public Library Board to have their books purchased and processed. The program is self-supporting, and it is hoped that the services can be broadened.

285. Southern Oregon Library Federation. "Proposal for Interlibrary Cooperation; An Action Program." Medford, Ore.: The Federation, May 1968. 6p. Mimeographed.

A large group of public, college, and high school librarians in five southern Oregon counties have formed the Southern Oregon Library Federation. The purpose is to achieve interlibrary cooperation through the exchange of materials, ideas, and services. The plan is to include a teletype communication system, efforts to open library facilities in the region to all persons, interlibrary lending and reference service to member libraries, free copy service, cooperative development of resources, expansion of centralized ordering and cataloging, development of subsystems among local communities, and continued library conferences. Further details of implementation and cost estimates are included in the proposal.

286. Anderson, Margaret. "Benefits and Economics of Interlibrary Cooperation—The Special Library Viewpoint," *News Notes of California Libraries* 63: 338-46 (Summer 1968).

The production of the *Houston List of Serials* is described along with the Regional Information and Communication Exchange (RICE) located at Rice University. RICE provides service to business and industry on a free basis.

Associated Science Libraries of San Diego involves academic, research, industrial, military, and public libraries in a cooperative effort including interlibrary loan, exchange of information about their collections, bibliographical assistance, study privileges to visitors, and referral service. An attempt is made to avoid duplication of expensive publications and to save time by providing rapid access to specialized collections in the area.

Boeing Company places a librarian on the University of Washington's campus to act as liaison and to handle all of the company's interlibrary loan requests. The California Institute of Technology Industrial Research Association and the M.I.T. Industrial Liaison Program are examples of industry paying universities for service. A similar arrangement exists at Stanford. Instances where special libraries provide service to high school students are also mentioned, but the success of these ventures has been mixed.

287. Cooley, Marguerite B. "Expanded Services Through the Federal Library Services and Construction Act," *Arizona Librarian* 25: 19-22 (Summer 1968).

The Arizona State Library Association received a grant to prepare a union list of periodicals; Library Services in Tucson received a grant for a Technical Services Center to serve the Tucson Public School District and the Tucson Public Library; Yuma City-County Library received a grant for an Associated Research Materials Center. The latter project involves Yuma City-County Library, Arizona Western College Library, and Yuma Proving Ground Technical Library.

288. "Library to Serve as Resource Center," North Dakota State Library Commission, *Library Notes and News* 81: 12 (Summer 1968).

Title III of LSCA has provided funds for the Minot (N.D.) Public Library to act as a resource center for school and public libraries in an 11-county section of northwestern North Dakota. Thirteen school and public libraries make up this "Northwest Library Federation." Libraries in the federation can request by mail or telephone interlibrary loan, copy, and reference services. The Minot Library will also serve as the agency for obtaining interlibrary loans from state, regional, and national sources. There will be roving collections of both fiction and nonfiction books, centralized cataloging, and processing of books purchased through the federation, a federation borrower's card, in-service training for trustees and librarians, and a film library for the use of member libraries.

289. Vormelker, Rose L. "Industrial Research and the Academic Library," *Journal of Education for Librarianship* 9: 60-71 (Summer 1968).

The article discusses the impact of the State Technical Services Act of 1965 as it affects increased use of academic libraries by industry. A dissertation on the subject by H. J. Mason is reviewed along with other pertinent literature.

Specific examples of cooperation in this problem area include programs at Stanford and Indiana Universities, the University of Pittsburgh, and the North Carolina Research Triangle (Duke University, University of North Carolina, and North Carolina University).

In New Jersey, a referral center receives inquiries and refers them to the library most able to answer them. The referral center began operation under the auspices of the New Jersey State Library and involves, in addition, Princeton University, the Public Library of Newark, and several industrial libraries.

290. "Summary of Nelson Associates' Study of the New York State Library's NYSILL Project and a Report of Decisions Relating to Continuation of the NYSILL Program," *Bookmark* 18: 363-71 (July 1968).

This is a summary of Nelson Associates' report on New York State's experimental interlibrary loan project, along with action taken on the recommendations of the study. A brief description of the program, which involved contracts between the state library and three area referral centers and nine subject referral centers, is given. These centers were to supplement the resources of the New York State Library for filling interlibrary loan requests.

The summary reports on the number of requests received, rates of success in filling them at various levels, origin of the requests, time in filling requests, and costs of providing the service. The program is being continued for an additional year with some modifications.

291. "1967-68 Service Programs and Projects: Federal Library Services and Construction Act," *From the California State Librarian* 47: 10-16 (29 July 1968).

The programs and projects financed in 1967-68 by the federal government, some of which are concerned with interlibrary cooperation, are described. The allocation grants under Titles I, II, III, and IV-B are outlined.

292. "School-Public Library Cooperation," *From the California State Librarian* 47: 28 (29 July 1968)

Three 1968 summer cooperative programs between school and public libraries in California are described.

In Daly City, the Jefferson Elementary School District and Daly City Public Library initiated joint operation of two children's libraries during summer vacation. School libraries provided the space and the books, the public library the staff. The two libraries are in schools some distance from public library branches, and provide service to children with relatively little access to the public library.

Hayward Public Library conducts a summer reading program jointly with five elementary schools in the Hayward Unified School District. The school district provides facilities and custodial services, and Hayward Public Library provides two library assistants at each school library, plus 1,000 additional books. The five school libraries are in elementary schools some distance from the public library.

The Fullerton Public Library has similar summer programs for preschool four-year-olds in which the public library furnishes the staff and the school library furnishes the books. These are planned especially for Spanish-speaking children and include some programs for mothers.

293. "State Library Processing Center Continues to Grow," *From the California State Librarian* 47: 30 (29 July 1968).

California's State Library Processing Center provides full processing for 30 public libraries plus one library system and card production for the Sacramento City/County Library. Three junior colleges have become members. Users are offered a choice of classification schemes.

294. "Reports from June 12 Morning Sessions: Public and School Librarians," *Bulletin of the Maine Library Association* 29: 7 (Aug. 1968).

The article discusses the development of library councils in the state of Maine, specifically the Waterville Area Council. The purposes of the council, which includes all types of librarians, are to promote cooperation and to provide a means for discussing common problems. Plans are to meet three times a year. The council is developing a directory of library resources in the area.

In Hancock County the council is developing lists of books, periodicals, and special tools and equipment which can be exchanged.

The Lewiston-Auburn Twin Cities Library Council will meet monthly and is open to anyone interested in library work. Committees have been formed to work on school assignments and on the creation of a directory of resources.

295. "Washington Metropolitan Area Libraries," *The Open Book* 7: 1 (Aug. 1968).

Forty thousand dollars from Title III funds have been awarded for a study of the feasibility of cooperation among libraries in the metropolitan Washington area. There is agreement among the eight public library systems of the area to establish a teletype communication and delivery service for interlibrary loans. "The National Library of Medicine and the consortium of five Washington, D.C., universities have indicated their willingness to be included in the interlibrary loan of books."

296. "Cooperative System of Art Libraries in Ohio," *The Ohio State University Libraries Notes* 4: no.7 (Sept. 1968).

The Ohio State University Libraries received a grant of $4,500 from the Ohio State Library Board to support a six-month study of the feasibility of establishing a cooperative network of art libraries in Ohio. The study was conducted by Jacqueline D. Sisson, and the final report of the study is listed in this bibliography as item 347.

Preliminary findings of the study indicated that Ohio has strong art libraries and that their respective resources are highly complementary. Lack of funds prevents individual libraries from acquiring all materials required for in-depth research. Establishing a plan for cooperative acquisitions was one of the aims of the study. Other areas in which the libraries indicated a willingness to cooperate are (1) more liberal lending policies for interlibrary loans; (2) reciprocal photocopying agreements; (3) exchange of lists of new acquisitions; (4) acceptance of responsibility for establishing subscriptions for serials not presently held.

The cooperating libraries are: Cincinnati Museum of Art, Cincinnati Public Library, University of Cincinnati, Cleveland Museum of Art, Cleveland Public Library, Oberlin College, The Ohio State University, Ohio University, and the Toledo Museum of Art. Denison University and Dominican College have also been invited to take part.

297. "MLC Initiates 'Instant Information' Service," *Mississippi Library News* 32: 141 (Sept. 1968).

The Mississippi Library Commission has a telephone reference system for the public libraries of Mississippi. A teletype system connects the commission with libraries at the University of Mississippi, Mississippi

State University, the University of Southern Mississippi, and the Mississippi Research and Development Center.

298. Mason, Diana. "Scarborough's Sin Spreads," *Ontario Library Review* 52: 146-47 (Sept. 1968).

The Scarborough Information Network (SIN) will eventually connect every information resource in the borough—schools, industry, hospitals, and others. Presently six Scarborough Public Library branches, the Administration Centre, and Centennial Community College are involved in the network. The principal use for the network is interlibrary loans. There is a good description of how the system works.

299. Southern Oregon Library Federation. "Proposal for a Regional Coordinator." Medford, Ore.: The Federation, Sept. 1968, 5p. Mimeographed.

This is a proposal for provision of a coordinator to help develop cooperative activities of the Southern Oregon Library Federation. It lists some of the past activities of the federation and some of the proposed activities, among them a region-wide computerized list of serials, and expansion of the Medford and Phoenix high school libraries for adult use.

300. "A New Breed of Cat," *Library Journal* 93: 3091-95 (15 Sept. 1968).

These observations on the workings of the Nassau Library System (Long Island, N.Y.) contain two references to attempts to involve the schools and the system in cooperative activities. The first was a pilot program for handling school library processing which was eventually dropped. The second was a Public Library/School Library Relations Program whose aim was to develop a number of ways in which schools and system member libraries could work together. Minimal success was reported.

301. "Telefacsimile Experiment Funded in Georgia," *Library Journal* 93: 3073 (15 Sept. 1968).

The experiment announced involves linking three college and one public library (Albany Public Library, Albany Junior College, and Southern Georgia College) by telefacsimile equipment. The libraries will attempt to improve serials services by pooling resources via telefacsimile. Xerox telecopiers are also being used in the project.

302. Burr, Elizabeth, "Interlibrary Cooperation Takes Planning," *Wisconsin Library Bulletin* 64: 353-54 (Sept.-Oct. 1968).

This article reports the funding of three proposals as part of Wisconsin's Title III program for fiscal 1968. In the Green Bay Metropolitan Area a computerized union list of serials is planned. In the Madison area, the University of Wisconsin Library School received a grant in support of "A Study to Ascertain Appropriate Cooperative Programs Among Types of Libraries in the Madison Metropolitan Area." The third is designated as Wisconsin Resource Interlace. Proposed by the Wisconsin Advisory Council on Library Development and the Library Advisory Committee of the Wisconsin Coordinating Council on Higher Education, its purpose is to plan for participation of library resources in Wisconsin in a mutually desirable statewide interlace.

303. Parsons, Arthur H., Jr. "Pratt Library Services to Teachers," *Baltimore Bulletin of Education* 36: 26-29 (Sept.-Oct. 1968).

The services of the Enoch Pratt Free Library not only to teachers but also to students are discussed here. Methods of cooperation between Pratt and the Baltimore public schools are outlined in some detail.

304. "Cooperation between Schools and Libraries," *Administrator's Digest* 3: 6 (Oct. 1968).

The De Soto Trail Regional Library in Georgia has a long-standing contract with the school systems in three counties to order, process, and catalog all books. For some 20 years, Evanston (Ill.) Public Library has been processing materials for the public schools. The Evanston Public Librarian also functioned as head librarian for the public school libraries. The Denver Public Library-Denver Public Schools Council, composed of representatives from the schools and the public library, was formed in 1958. Various cooperative efforts have been initiated as a result. The Cuyahoga County Public Library provides professional assistance and technical processing service to 294 public schools in the Cleveland area. The Salt Lake County (Utah) Library System conducted 2,100 classes in the use of libraries for school children in the 1966-67 school year.

305. Murdoch, Faith T. "The Relationship of the School Library to the Young Adult Librarian in the Public Library," *Library Trends* 17: 183-90 (Oct. 1968).

The "liaison librarian" is a new type in the public library systems of Nioga and Westchester, New York, and also in Prince George's County,

Maryland. Liaison librarians "zero in on the problems most often identified as stumbling blocks to youth. Working directly with and through school librarians, they provide channels of communication which alleviate the misunderstandings which too often exist between the public library and the schools. Through direct and frequent contacts with the schools, they provide a climate of understanding and good will which fosters an ideal partnership."

306. "DCLA Notes," *D. C. Libraries* 39: 83-84 (Fall 1968).

A plan to produce by computer a cooperative book catalog of the holdings of the Fairfax County Public Library and the Northern Virginia Community College libraries has been approved by Virginia under a Title III grant. The computer programming will allow other libraries to join in the project with no program change.

307. Holt, Raymond M. "How Many Drops to Fill the Bucket," *News Notes of California Libraries* 63: 455-66 (Fall 1968).

This address to the Governor's Conference concerns cooperative activity in general, but contains a reference to the Black Gold Library System's cooperative arrangement with Moorpark College. The college is to be tied to the system by teletype. Another system activity is a cooperative program with a state hospital.

308. Humphry, John A. "New York Looks Ahead: A Challenge to California?" *News Notes of California Libraries* 63: 441-53 (Fall 1968).

In an address to the California Governor's Conference on Libraries, New York's Assistant Commissioner for Libraries describes some of his state's cooperative library activities.

Among them is the New York Metropolitan Reference and Research Library Agency, Inc. (METRO), one of nine reference and research systems. Its membership includes 70 different libraries—four public library systems, a number of large college and university libraries, research libraries, and special libraries. METRO has sponsored or plans to sponsor such projects as the assembling of a specialized list of consultants, centralized storage of lesser used materials, an interlibrary communication network, an interlibrary training and discussion program, and an interlibrary transportation and messenger service. A study has also been made to identify the needs of users of scientific and technical collections in the metropolitan area in order to design a program that will more nearly meet their needs.

Other state projects include the state library's efforts to include the New York Academy of Medicine in a special subject interlibrary loan system.

A key element in the reference and research program is an interlibrary loan pilot project involving public, special, and academic libraries. A number of libraries are under contract to the state library to provide materials for interlibrary loan which the state library is unable to provide.

309. Harm, Melvin P. "A Description and Interim Report of the 'Electronic Information Sharing Distribution Network' among Four Libraries in South Georgia." Albany, Ga.: Albany Jr. College, Nov. 1968. 9p. Mimeographed.

This is a general report about the telefacsimile communications project started in 1968 by the Albany Junior College, the Albany State College, the Albany Public Library, and the South Georgia College in Douglas. The objectives, rationale, planned activities, and the time table for this cooperative system are described. It was felt that interlibrary service could be given faster, more accurately, and not just for a patron with a "crisis." Equipment, supplies, and expenditures of the project are outlined. The public was informed of the new service through video tapes on the local television station, demonstrations, and news releases. The project will run at least through 30 June 1969, and has been funded through Title III Library Services and Construction Act.

310. "PPL Honors ICC Cards," *Peoria Public Library Staff Spokesman* 14: 6 (7 Nov. 1968).

The Peoria Public Library Board and the administration of Illinois Central Junior College have agreed that Peoria Public Library will honor the cards of students of Illinois Central Junior College. The students will use their plastic identification cards with the public library's Gaylord charging machines. The college will assume responsibility for the return, loss, or damage of public library material.

311. "Intertype Teletype Network Set Up in Delaware," *Library Journal* 93: 4605 (15 Dec. 1968).

Funds from Title III of LSCA have made possible a program called the Delaware Rapid Interlibrary Loan and Reference Service (DRILL). The

University of Delaware is coordinating this statewide teletype network which provides for the exchange of reference and interlibrary loan information among university, college, and public libraries. Resources outside the state will be contacted through the university.

1969

312. Evansville (Ind.) Public Library and Vanderburgh County Public Library. *Periodicals in Evansville Libraries: 1969.* 42p.

A list of periodicals in the Evansville Public Library; the Evansville State Hospital; the Clifford Memorial Library; the Chemistry Library and the Physics Department of the University of Evansville; Indiana State University, Evansville Campus; the Professional Materials Center of the Evansville Vanderburgh School Corporation; and the Willard Library.

313. Hildebrand, Lorraine, and Aiken, Richard S., eds. *A Bibliography of Afro-American Print and Non-Print Resources in Libraries of Pierce County, Washington.* Tacoma: Tacoma Community College Library, 1969. 116p.

Thirty-three libraries cooperated in this project sponsored by the Tacoma Area Urban Coalition Education Task Force. The bibliography is designed to make Afro-American resources in the county accessible to the Education Task Force for use by the public; to satisfy the growing demand for materials for use in "black studies" courses; and to provide checklists for use in the preparation of other bibliographies and lists of resources in other parts of the country.

The bibliography contains a union list of print and nonprint resources and checklists of black authors and black artists, musicians, actors, and other entertainers.

314. Martin, Lowell A. *Library Response to Urban Change: A Study of the Chicago Public Library.* Chicago: American Library Assn., 1969. 313p.

Martin includes many recommendations which may lead to interlibrary cooperation. He recommends the formation of a Metropolitan Library Council to plan for a library network to serve the greater Chicago area. A senior administrative officer in the Chicago Public Library is to be assigned responsibility for "developing and maintaining productive working relationships with other libraries of all types." A working agreement between the public library and the Chicago Board of Education is called for to include an experimental joint school-public library and to locate regional library centers in proposed cultural-educational complexes. In addition, a research-level "Bibliographic Center" and a new "Library Information Center" would link resources in a city-wide information network which eventually would provide facsimile transmission among the "reference and research" libraries in the Illinois system.

315. Nelson Associates, Inc. *Interlibrary Loan in New York State*. New York: Nelson Associates, Inc., Feb. 1969. 300p.

This is an extensive report of the findings of a study of Phase II of the New York State Library's statewide reference and research interlibrary loan network (NYSILL). The study was designed to provide "a detailed review of the performance and operations of the several systems in operation," to examine interlibrary loans outside these systems, and to review future developments, particularly technological ones, which might affect NYSILL.

In addition to providing background information on the development of the network, thee report presents findings on the character of information needs in the state, the nature of NYSILL requests, the operation of NYSILL, a statistical analysis of the system, and an overall evaluation of interlibrary loan service in the state.

The major finding is that the system is working well, and it is recommended that the program be made permanent. A number of recommendations are made for improvements in the system.

316. Nelson Associates, Inc. *Public Library Systems in the United States; A Survey of Multijurisdictional Systems*. By Nelson Associates for the Public Library Association, American Library Association. Chicago: American Library Assn., 1969. 368p.

This comprehensive survey of system development in the United States is concerned primarily with public libraries. Cooperative arrangements with other types of libraries come most frequently in the areas of interlibrary loan and reference service. In the case studies presented there is an example of involvement with school libraries in the Wayne County (Mich.) Federated Library System and with industry in the Memphis and Shelby County (Tenn.) Public Libraries.

The need for greater leadership in working with the administrators of other educational agencies to develop more effective total library programs is pointed out.

317. Nolting, Orin F. *Mobilizing Library Resources for Effective Service*. Chicago: American Library Assn., 1969. 20p.

This paper was prepared as background material for a meeting sponsored by six ALA divisions at the 1969 Annual Conference. While not concerned with specific examples of cooperation, it is included here because of its attempt to pinpoint barriers to effective cooperation among different types of libraries. Part of the paper is devoted to reporting discussions held on this subject at ten one-day meetings in different parts of the country. Barriers identified are grouped into five categories: (1) psychological barriers; (2) lack of information and experience; (3) traditional and historical barriers; (4) physical and geographical barriers; (5) legal and administrative barriers. Various aspects of these categories are discussed and a number of alternative solutions proposed.

318. River Bend Library System. *Annual Report, 1968-69.* Moline, Ill.: The System, 1969.

This Illinois public library system provides catalog cards to John Deere and Company for 30¢ per set. This system also cooperates with Black Hawk College in a plan wherein the college provides back-up reference service for the system. Lack of use of this latter service has forced re-evaluation of the program.

319. Crawford, Carolyn. "Cooperation Between School Libraries and other Types of Libraries," in Cora E. Thomassen, ed., *Cooperation Between Types of Libraries: The Beginnings of a State Plan for Library Services in Illinois,* p.47-59. (Allerton Park Institute, no.15) Urbana: Univ. of Illinois, Graduate School of Library Science, 1969.

This address to the Allerton Conference outlines some of the landmark achievements in cooperative ventures involving school libraries. The 1963 Conference Within a Conference, and the 1966 ALA Young Adult Services Division Pre-Conference in Library Programs for Disadvantaged Youth are mentioned along with the impact of federal aid programs.

There is a discussion of several state level policy statements concerning the function of school and public libraries and standards for their operation.

Also included is a very detailed description of Hawaii's unique centralized library system under the State Department of Education. The system includes the State Library, all public libraries, all public school libraries, and the Central Processing Center; the latter serves both school and public libraries. A description of both recommended and actual cooperative activities is provided.

320. Shank, Russell. "Cooperation Between Special Libraries and Other Types of Libraries." in Cora E. Thomassen, ed., *Cooperation Between Types of Libraries: The Beginnings of a State Plan for Library Services in Illinois,* p.60-72. (Allerton Park Institute, no.15) Urbana: Univ. of Illinois, Graduate School of Library Science, 1969.

Most cooperation between special and any other libraries is informal and consists chiefly of interlibrary loan agreements. The tendency seems to be for special libraries to cooperate with similar kinds of libraries. The author believes that the building of systems and networks among libraries will give better service to special libraries and other libraries as well. Some specific forms of cooperation such as Houston's Regional Information and Communication Exchange (RICE) are discussed as are cooperative proposals in Connecticut and New York City. Medical libraries (hospital, academic, research, and the like) have been especially active in cooperation. Suggestions to implement further cooperation are given.

321. Vann, Sarah K. "Cooperation Between Different Types of Libraries in Technical Services," in Cora E. Thomassen, ed., *Cooperation Between Types of Libraries: The Beginnings of a State Plan for Library Services in Illinois,* p.12-35. (Allerton Park Institute, no.15) Urbana: Univ. of Illinois, Graduate School of Library Science, 1969.

The author describes a number of types of centralized processing arrangements which are possible and then reports on centralized processing activities under way in this country. A good review of the literature concerning centralized processing is provided together with a list of questions which can serve as a guide to anyone considering such a program.

322. Wright, Donald E. "Cooperation Between Types of Libraries in Illinois Today," in Cora E. Thomassen, ed., *Cooperation Between Types of Libraries: The Beginnings of a State Plan for Library Services in Illinois,* p.36-46. (Allerton Park Institute, no.15) Urbana: Univ. of Illinois, Graduate School of Library Science, 1969.

The author attempts to review instances of cooperation between different types of libraries in Illinois. After a search of the literature revealed few examples, the author sent a questionnaire to 500 libraries asking if they had been involved in or had discussed cooperative activities with other types of libraries. Of the 296 replies received, 172 libraries answered no to both questions. For those libraries which answered yes, a list of some of the activities is given.

A fuller discussion of school-public library cooperation as it has existed in Evanston (Ill.) is also given.

323. Burns, Robert W. "The Pacific Northwest Federation of Forestry Libraries—An Experiment in Regional Cooperation," *Pacific Northwest Library Association Quarterly* 33: 20-25 (Winter 1969).

The Pacific Northwest Federation of Forestry Libraries was conceived as an experimental network to test the hypothesis that regional cooperation in the acquisition of library materials can work at a disciplinary level even though each cooperating unit remains autonomous and may have other areas of interest. The goals of the federation are to (1) identify and consider for purchase all forestry materials not in the area; (2) encourage a systematic effort to close the gaps identified; and (3) develop future plans for fitting this regional group into a national network. Membership includes state, special, university, and federal libraries.

324. "California State Library Report, 1967-68," *News Notes of California Libraries* 64: 3-17 (Winter 1969).

This annual report of the California State Library makes brief mention of several cooperative projects involving different types of libraries. The California Union Catalog reports the addition of the first special library to its 77 contributors, and the State Library Processing Center notes the addition of the first college library to its list of 30 subscribers.

Title III grants have been made for a cooperative information network for all libraries in the Black Gold Cooperative Library System area, for the extension of service to business and industry in Fresno County, and for an interstate program involving one county in California and one in Nevada. No details of these plans are given.

325. "Action in Missoula," *Montana State Library Newsletter* 4: 1 (Jan. 1969).

As a result of the Marvin study, *A Plan for Library Cooperation in Missoula County, Montana,* the Missoula Area Library Club has been formed with membership open to librarians, media center specialists, and others interested in interlibrary cooperation and development.

326. Becker, Joseph. "Information Network Prospects in the United States," *Library Trends* 17: 306-17 (Jan. 1969).

Becker gives a good introduction to the library cooperation of the future, network systems. "The concept of a dynamic network involving all types of libraries has been advanced in Washington, New York, California, and other states."

327. Buddington, William S. "Interrelations Among Special Libraries," *Library Quarterly* 39: 64-77 (Jan. 1969).

One example of cooperation between special and other type libraries is the Associated Science Libraries of San Diego. This group includes 19 libraries—7 corporations, 3 universities and colleges, 1 public library, 3 government agencies, and 5 research and cultural organizations. The purposes are: "(1) pooling library materials and librarians' services by facilitating interlibrary loans, exchange of information about collections, bibliographic assistance, visitor's study privileges, and referral services; (2) avoidance of unnecessary duplication of publications; and (3) saving of time by rapid ascertaining of and access to specialized collections in the San Diego area."

There are also special information centers at Rice and Southern Methodist Universities and a union list of science and technology periodicals in the Houston area. Cooperation schemes involving public, academic, industrial, and research libraries in Great Britain are discussed; there were 32 such groups by 1966.

328. Cory, John M. "The Network in a Major Metropolitan Center (METRO, New York)," *Library Quarterly* 39: 90-98 (Jan. 1969).

The purpose of the New York Metropolitan Reference and Research Library Agency (METRO) is to: "Improve reference and research library service in the New York Metropolitan area by promoting and facilitating utilization of existing resources and by developing additional resources." There are over 50 member libraries in METRO, including two in New Jersey, and there are almost 400 library outlets and cataloged collections of nearly 25 million volumes. METRO is truly cooperation among different types of libraries—university, college, seminary, special, and public. The bylaws of METRO do permit business corporations and other profit organizations to affiliate as corporate members, but without voting privileges. This article is an excellent summary of the legal and organizational status, history, present activities, and future prospects of METRO.

329. Gaines, Ervin J. "The Large Municipal Library as a Network," *Library Quarterly* 39: 41-51 (Jan. 1969).

Believing that there will be a steady shift of children's library service from the public library to the schools, and that the schools will take over some of the services traditionally accorded the public library, the Minneapolis Public Library has made an agreement with the Board of Education for a junior high school to provide year-round service to the community.

330. Purdy, G. Flint. "Interrelationships among Public, School and Academic Libraries," *Library Quarterly* 39: 52-63 (Jan. 1969).

An outline is included which goes into great detail on current programs and plans for cooperation. The eight main categories of the outline are: union catalogs and lists, cooperative development of resources, sharing resources in terms of use, communication, centralized processing, cooperatively sponsored planning and surveys, cooperative storage, and cooperative computer centers. Examples of each type of cooperation are provided in the outline.

Most of the rest of the article is devoted to a description of examples of cooperative efforts in Michigan. The state's evolving network of library systems is described along with Washington State's plan for an information network.

331. "Student Library Resource Requirements in Philadelphia," *Pennsylvania Library Association Bulletin* 24: 51-53 (Jan. 1969).

This article announced a unique research project supported by a U.S. Office of Education grant to the Philadelphia School District. The purposes of the study are (1) to determine library resource requirements by all elementary and secondary school students in Philadelphia; and (2) on the basis of that information to outline the respective roles of the Free Library and the school libraries in providing the needed resources, including joint and centralized facilities and technological systems. The study has the support and sponsorship of the public, parochial, and private schools of Philadelphia and the Free Library.

332. Forrester, George. "The Scarborough Information Network, Canada," *Unesco Bulletin for Libraries* 23: 22-24, 45 (Jan.-Feb. 1969).

Early in 1968 Scarborough Public Library (Canada) began operation of a teletype network connecting the branches of the library and the union catalog in the Administration Centre of the Scarborough Public Library. The purpose of the system is to facilitate interlibrary loans among the branches. In March 1968, Centennial College of Applied Arts and Technology in Scarborough joined the system to have access to the holdings of Scarborough Public Library and to facilitate future cooperation in acquisitions. In September 1968, a high school was connected with the circuit. An additional teletype machine, installed in October 1968, enables borrowers to have access to books in the public libraries of metropolitan Toronto.

333. Hoeffgen, Helen. "Branch Library Programs: Operation Shoestring Budget," *Wilson Library Bulletin* 43: 545-51 (Feb. 1969).

This article describes some of the problems faced in getting adults to use the resources of a public library branch located in a school and what was done in Flint (Mich.) to solve the problem.

The series of programs held in the Civic Park Branch included lectures of interest to adults, films, and concerts, all of which were followed by tours of the library facilities.

334. Howard, Edward N. "Interlibrary Cooperation in the Indianapolis Metropolitan Area," *Library Occurrent* 23: 16-18 (Feb. 1969).

Howard examines informal cooperation between all types of libraries in the Indianapolis (Ind.) metropolitan area. He finds that 59 percent of the 39 libraries studied borrowed materials from other libraries in the area. Publicly supported institutions were the major sources of borrowed materials, with business and industrial libraries providing only 9 percent of the materials loaned. However, the Science and Technology Division of Indianapolis Public Library maintains a union list of specialized periodical holdings in corporate libraries. The Special Libraries Association, Indiana Chapter, was influential in establishing the union list.

335. "Community Trips to the Public Library," *Library Journal* 94: 621, 638 (15 Feb. 1969).

A third grade teacher uses public library materials in a program of individualized reading instruction. Continued use of the library with voluntary independent reading interests is the goal.

336. "County Reference Library Chartered in New York," *Library Journal* 94: 706 (15 Feb. 1969).

Nassau County Reference Library will serve 53 public and several academic and special libraries in Nassau County, Long Island, as a part of the John F. Kennedy Educational Civic and Cultural Center.

337. "D.C. Area Libraries Form Interstate Link," *Library Journal* 94: 707 (15 Feb. 1969).

Eight public library systems in the Washington, D.C., area will link their resources with the National Library of Medicine and the libraries of Georgetown, Howard, George Washington, and Catholic Universities. Daily deliveries to readers from the various libraries will be provided with book requests being coordinated by the Montgomery County Department of Public Libraries. Service was scheduled to begin 20 April 1969.

338. "Regional Center of the '70's Seen in Pittsburgh Study," *Library Journal* 94: 704 (15 Feb. 1969).

This article is a brief preview of *The Regional Library Center in the 1970's, A Concept Paper* by Thomas Minder. It has special reference to the Pittsburgh Regional Center but has application to cooperative library organization in general. The author sees a facility which serves as an adjunct or special department of each library using it. The idea is to relieve member libraries of most clerical work, technical processing, storage of lesser used materials, interlibrary loans, transactions with other library networks, bibliographic files, and computer technology.

339. "Delivery Service Begins for College Libraries," *ALA Bulletin* 63: 296-97 (March 1969).

The Southeastern New York Library Resources Council has established a delivery service for twelve area college libraries and two major public libraries in the area. "Other cooperative programs have included the payment of all telephone toll charges among college and research libraries in the Hudson Valley and the reimbursal of all photocopying expenses in interlibrary loan transactions. The Council also publishes finding lists and sponsors training institutes."

340. "Drill in Delaware," *ALA Bulletin* 63: 299 (March 1969).

Delaware Rapid Interlibrary Loan and Reference Service (DRILL), founded with LSCA Title III funds, is a teletypewriter network for the exchange of reference and interlibrary loan information among public, college, and university libraries in the state. The University of Delaware is acting as coordinator for the project.

341. "Rural Reciprocity." *School Library Journal* 94: 1267 (March 1969).

The cooperative efforts between the Madera County (Calif.) Library and local schools are described. Bus service was provided from three schools to the county library branch. The program was continued for five years until each school was able to open its own library.

342. Shuman, Bruce A. "WATS Happening in North Carolina," *Library Journal* 94: 945-47 (1 March 1969).

Direct telephone communication between public libraries and the state library's Reference Services Division, for the purpose of both reference service and interlibrary loans has been established in North Carolina.
    A TWX hookup with the statewide union catalog in Chapel Hill is used for location of items not found in the state library catalog or the state library location file and for contact with locations in other states.

343. "Intertype Cooperation," *Library Journal* 94: 1089 (15 March 1969).

Public, academic, and research librarians in the Mid-Hudson Valley of New York will visit each other's libraries for a week at a time to study the operations and resources of cooperating institutions. Two public librarians will visit the Franklin D. Roosevelt Library in Hyde Park, while two others visit Vassar College Library.

344. Neff, Evaline B. "Rochester Regional Research Library Council," *Bookmark* 28: 214-19 (April 1969).

The Rochester Regional Research Library Council is a formal cooperative structure which includes many different types of libraries—a university, colleges, community colleges, schools of divinity, hospitals, museums, a historical society, a law library, a dental library, and company and industrial libraries. The two major libraries are the University of Rochester and the Rochester Public Library. "All but one of the libraries will honor requests for interlibrary loans and/or photocopies."

Total holdings of Council libraries were 2,733,880 monographs and 28,935 serial subscriptions as of December 1967. The University of Rochester and the Rochester Public Library are reimbursed for supplying interlibrary loan and photocopying services. A translation service was initiated in January 1969. Committees for a regional union list of serials and for coordinated acquisitions are at work. A census coordinating committee has been organized "to formulate a plan to establish and operate a regional center for the dissemination of census information utilizing the U.S. Bureau of the Census computer tapes."

345. Pfoutz, Daniel R. "PENNTAP," *Library Journal* 94: 1589-91 (15 April 1969).

The Carnegie Library of Pittsburgh has a mobile research library called the PENNTAP van (Pennsylvania Technical Assistance Program) which seeks to aid business and industry in the location and provision of engineering and technical information. PENNTAP is cosponsored by the federal and state Departments of Commerce and, although designed to meet the needs of small and medium-sized business firms, is open to any business or industry. Institutions of higher education in Pennsylvania provide the special services required. The model van operates in the fashion of a bookmobile, visiting business firms and industrial plants with literature most frequently required by business and industry.

346. "Miscellany," *College and Research Library News* 30: 171-72 (May 1969).

Minnesota Interlibrary Teletype Experiment (MINITEX), was announced by the University of Minnesota Library in December 1968. This two-year pilot project is financed by state and federal (LSCA) funds and a grant from the Louis and Maud Hill Family Foundation. The purpose of MINITEX is to obtain cost, volume, and operational data that will provide a basis for developing recommendations for a long-range statewide interlibrary service program. The participating libraries were carefully selected to represent college, state college, junior college, university branch campus, and public library needs for access to the resources of the University Library. The grants for the pilot project total $103,200.

347. Sisson, Jacqueline D. "Final Report of a Study of a Cooperative System of Ohio Art Libraries, May 1968-April 1969." Columbus: The Ohio State Univ. Libraries, 2 May 1969. 42p. Mimeographed.

This is the final report of the study described in preliminary form in item 296 of this bibliography. The introduction to the report states that not only was the feasibility of such a network investigated, but that concrete steps toward establishing the network were taken during the course of the study. The participating libraries have formed an organization, Art Research Libraries of Ohio (ARLO), and have agreed to accept responsibility for acquisitions in specialized areas.

The chronology of the study, results of bibliographic checks, the relative strengths of the collections, interlibrary loan and photocopying policies, cooperative book selection, and problems associated with the need for a union catalog are discussed in the report.

Recommendations deal with problems of funding, communication, exchange of catalog cards, establishment of reference and bibliographic services for member libraries, publication of bibliographies, and several other areas.

348. Lightfoot, Robert M., Jr. "Library Cooperation Peoria Style," *Illinois Libraries* 51: 533-37 (June 1969).

Lightfoot tells of the arrangement between Bradley University (Peoria, Ill.) and the Peoria Public Library whereby university students have access to the public library's collection. Earlier practice had required a fee of students who lived outside the city limits and serious problems had been encountered in the return of public library materials.

Both libraries use the Gaylord charging system and any Bradley student may borrow materials using his university identification card. Public library materials may be returned either to the public library or the university library. Overdue notices are sent to the university where names and addresses are supplied and forms mailed. Failure to return materials or pay fines results in withholding of grades and transcript.

The plan provides additional materials for the students, thus easing pressure on university facilities while eliminating the problem of delinquency.

APPENDIX

Many of the responses to the request for information on interlibrary cooperation came in the form of letters accompanied by descriptive brochures and pamphlets. Since the format of these materials presented some difficulties in entering them in the main body of the bibliography, they are presented in this appendix. The entries are arranged by country and state and then by city, area, or project name. The numbering of the items has been continued from the main body of the bibliography.

Nigeria

349. Yaba, Lagos

On 29 September 1969, the Lagos Special Libraries Information Service (LASLIS) was formally inaugurated to coordinate the resources of educational, commercial, and industrial libraries in the Lagos area. The headquarters of LASLIS is located in the Yaba College of Technology Library. Effective interlibrary service is the major objective.

United States (Nationwide)

350. Library Network Directors' Group. "Directory of Library Consortia and Cooperative Projects." Draft.

This directory was assembled by the Organizational Committee of the ad hoc Library Network Directors' Group to "provide the attendees of the Atlantic City meeting [1969] with some preliminary data upon which to base its decisions for permanent organizational status, group objectives, purposes, organizational name and membership criteria; second, it may serve as a basis for future more comprehensive editions if a need is evident." The draft contains a good deal of information about such organizations as the Bibliographical Center for Research — Rocky

Mountain Region and the Rochester Regional Research Library Council, including personnel and types of activities carried on or under consideration.

Arizona

351. Tucson

With the aid of Title III-LSCA funds the Tucson Public Library and the Tucson public schools are exploring the possibility of combining technical services operations. A feasibility study has been made which concluded that the project would be workable. The second stage involves the implementation of the recommendations and the actual combination of the operations. A committee of two persons from each of the two groups involved has made recommendations for the design of the program.

California

352. Black Gold Cooperative Library System

The Black Gold System, with headquarters at the San Luis Obispo County Library, San Luis Obispo, is cooperating with Moorpark College and is anticipating cooperation with 15 other libraries of various types—state college, university, small private, junior colleges, special libraries, and institutional libraries.

Moorpark College has been tied into the system's teletype Information Service and has been furnished with the system's book form catalogs. The two have cooperated in publishing a union list of serials.

353. Long Beach

Close cooperation has existed between the schools and the public library; a brochure describing these activities is in process of compilation.

354. Sacramento Area Library Organization (SALO)

This group had its origin in a meeting of area librarians called by the librarian of the Sacramento County Office of Education to discuss mutual problems. From an initial attendance of about ten people the group has grown to a mailing list of about 200 people and an average meeting attendance of 40. The organization invites the participation of librarians, library aides, volunteer mothers, and other interested persons. Meetings centered around a variety of discussion topics are held at different libraries in the area.

One of the group's most popular and successful projects has been a "Booknik-of-the-Month Contest" in which prizes have been awarded to students who submitted the best book review or discussion of an author.

The county schools office continues to assist the organization.

Colorado

355. Aurora Library Council

Meetings of school, public, and special librarians in Aurora are held every two months to discuss problems and to plan cooperative service for students. A brochure describes the resources and facilities of the participating libraries, the services and responsibilities of school and public libraries, and some of the ways in which teachers and librarians can work together.

Connecticut

356. Connecticut State Library

In 1968 the Connecticut State Library published the *Directory of Subject Strengths in Connecticut Libraries*. Public, academic, school, and special libraries contributed information for the list.

357. New London County

The Waterford Public Library is among the fourteen public, two academic, and four special libraries in New London County (Conn.) which have formed an informal organization and published the *Union List of Periodicals, New London County Libraries, November, 1968*.

Florida

358. Orlando Public Library—University of Florida Libraries

In 1968, a $25,000 federal grant made it possible to establish a facsimile transmission service between the Orlando Public Library's Business, Science and Technology Department and the University of Florida's Technical Information Division. Orlando businessmen and students of urban studies are seen as important users of the service.

Illinois

359. Kankakee

As a result of the Allerton Park Conference, "Cooperation between Types of Libraries," Kankakee Community College, Kankakee Junior

College, Olivet Nazarene College, Armour Technical Library, and Kankakee Public Library have been discussing plans for cooperation projects. A union list of periodicals is one of the group's early accomplishments.

Indiana

360. Indianapolis

In 1968 the Bureau of Public Discussion of Indiana University published a *Directory of Libraries and Specialized Collections in the Indianapolis Metropolitan Area.* Libraries that contributed to the directory include college, university, public, business, industrial, government agency, and nonprofit association libraries.

361. Terre Haute

In 1968 a preliminary draft of *Libraries and Specialized Collections in the Vigo County Area* was circulated in pamphlet format before publication. The directory also reports on services which are available to patrons. Church, college, university, public, school, and special libraries contributed information for the directory.

Kentucky

362. Campbellsville College, Campbellsville

The Campbellsville College provides high school librarians with referral cards which may be used by Campbellsville high school students when they are unable to obtain needed materials from the school or public libraries.

363. Greater Louisville Technical Referral Center

This center is a state technical service center engaged in cooperative work with industrial, academic, and public libraries. A union list of serials has been published, work on a card catalog of newly acquired monographic materials has begun, TWX has been installed for interlibrary loan and referral use, a photocopy exchange pool has been established, and television tapes for instructional use in the area of interlibrary loans have been prepared. A computer-based reference service is offered to both academic and industrial personnel.

The Technical Referral Center is also working with Metroversity, an organization composed of academic libraries in the city but with some participation by public and special librarians. The center is compiling a union list of serials for this group and is planning a central automated serials system.

Massachusetts

364. Needham

The purpose of the brochure, *Focus on Libraries; A Combined Policy Statement of the Needham Public Library and the Needham Public Schools* (Needham, Mass., 1965), is to explain the interaction of the public and school libraries in Needham. Grade school children visit the public library, and public librarians tell stories in the schools and give instructions in public library use. Both grade and high school teachers are asked to give advance notice of assignments to librarians. The public library cooperates with the schools on a summer reading program and a young adult librarian works with junior and senior high school librarians. The public library actively encourages use by students.

365. Southbridge

An informal but close pattern of cooperation exists among the public library, the school libraries, both public and parochial, and Jacob Edwards Memorial Library, the research library of American Optical Company, in Southbridge. Interlibrary lending and referral are common and a number of informal agreements on acquisitions have grown up over the years.

Old Sturbridge Village, within ten miles, has a research library specializing in American history, 1790-1840, to which patrons can be referred. In turn it relies on the public library for more general bibliographic tools. A similar arrangement exists with Nichols College which specializes in business and forestry.

These resources, together with cooperation from teachers, have proved adequate in providing material for students completing class assignments.

366. Springfield

Thirteen libraries in the Springfield area contributed to the completion of the second edition of the *Union List of Periodicals in Libraries in the Greater Springfield, Massachusetts Area*. The holdings of junior college, college, medical, insurance, law, industrial, and public libraries are represented in this automated listing.

367. West Concord—Concord Free Library, Fowler Branch

Fowler Branch of the Concord Free Library cooperated with the Concord Public Schools in an experimental Individualized Learning Center for selected students in grades one through five. The center had no library of its own so the public library supplied materials and a special librarian to work with the students. Minor library problems were resolved but, although successful from the library's viewpoint, the project has not been continued.

Michigan

368. Olivet

In the absence of a public library Olivet College extends its services free of charge to high school students, residents of Olivet, and two other nearby towns. High school classes are brought to the college library for instruction in the use of the library.

Minnesota

369. Cooperating Libraries in Consortium (Minneapolis-St. Paul)

The libraries of seven private colleges—Augsburg, Bethel, Concordia, Macalester, Hamline, St. Catherine, and St. Thomas—and the Hill Reference Library in the Twin Cities have agreed to work together through an organization called Cooperating Libraries in Consortium. Annual contributions from each library hopefully will support a program in joint acquisition of materials and joint storage of little-used materials. The greatest effect will be the availability to the colleges of more library materials and services through cooperation.

Montana

370. Missouri Area Library Club

The Missoula Area Library Club was organized to foster library development through interlibrary cooperation and is composed of representatives of university, public and county, public and parochial high school, elementary school, and special libraries; also included is an instructional materials center. The club holds informal discussions on cooperation. Concentration thus far has been on improvement of interlibrary loan service.

Nebraska

371. Lincoln

Libraries and Lessons is a pamphlet prepared at the request of the Lincoln Library Board and the Lincoln Board of Education. The pamphlet was designed to point out "problems encountered in assisting students and to offer suggestions for a more efficient use of all library facilities." It includes sections on teaching library use, an outline for library orientation, planning for individual use, book selection, and a listing of other community resources available to teachers and students.

Another instance of cooperation has been the combination of genealogical materials of the university and public libraries with those of the State Historical Society Library.

New England

372. Regional Planning Committee of the New England Library Association.

The Regional Planning Committee has compiled *Directory of Cooperative Library Activities in New England,* scheduled for publication in late 1969.

New Mexico

373. A report from the New Mexico State Library (Santa Fe, N.M.) describes the activities and reactions to the State Library Demonstration Traveling Library Center. The project was aimed at upgrading the knowledge and training of people giving library service to children and young people in the state. A questionnaire was used to evaluate the project and to help consider whether it be continued as a means of training library personnel. The project was sponsored cooperatively by the Department of Education, the State Library, and several other service divisions.

New York

374. Brooklyn

The Brooklyn Public Library and Brooklyn Polytechnic Institute joined in preparing *Business and Management Research: A Guide to the Brooklyn Public Library Business Library for Students of Business and Management.* Periodical and newspaper holdings, indexing services, census reports, directories, maps, vertical file information, and a variety of other resources are listed.

375. North Salem

The North Salem Free Library works closely with the schools in the villages it serves. Acquisitions are coordinated and, as the school libraries have improved, the public library has shifted its purchases to recreational and supplementary materials and away from instructional materials. Feeling unable to support two reference collections in the town, the public library maintains a small basic collection while the school concentrates on building a more extensive collection which is available to both students and adults.

376. Southeastern New York Library Resources Council

The council, with offices in Poughkeepsie, includes 14 academic libraries, one presidential library, and two public library systems. The council sponsors a delivery service for members, reimburses them for photocopies they supply to other member libraries, and maintains a telephone credit card for use in interlibrary loan and reference requests. The council has sponsored a number of publications, among them a union list of serials in the area and a number of directories and guides to resources.

Ohio

377. Southwestern Ohio

An "Ad Hoc Media Expo 1969 Conference" was held for people in southwestern Ohio, and included participants from public schools, private schools, colleges, the university, industry, the State Department of Education, the State Library, and the Diocese of Columbus. The purpose of the conference was to emphasize "the need for an immediate and closer look at the future of Instructional Materials" in southwestern Ohio. The impetus and planning for the institute came from the Library Education Committee of the Consortium (Miami Valley).

Pennsylvania

378. Area College Library Cooperative Program of Central Pennsylvania (ACLCP)

The Area College Library Cooperative Program (ACLCP) is basically for the libraries of undergraduate colleges in central Pennsylvania, but the Pennsylvania State Library at Harrisburg is a supporting member. The highlights of the program are the development of a coordinated acquisitions program, tentative agreements on the area of concentration in each college, the provision of free photocopies of material, and a union list of complete periodical holdings of all member libraries.

379. Northeastern Pennsylvania Bibliographic Center

The Northeastern Pennsylvania Bibliographic Center (NEPBC), established in 1956, is a cooperative program involving 13 major libraries—7 academic, 4 public, and 2 special—for the purpose of making more books available through a union catalog of books. The union catalog, maintained at Kings College (Wilkes-Barre), shows the location of 263,000 titles.

In 1959 a union list of serials of the participating libraries was prepared; in 1962 the list was changed to a computer format.

Other activities include demonstration teletype and TWX projects tying the center to the Union Library Catalog of Pennsylvania in Philadelphia, and cooperation in building collections of both print and nonprint materials.

380. Pittsburgh

A workshop sponsored in May 1969 by the Southwest District Chapter of the Pennsylvania Library Association dealt with school and public library cooperation. Much of the discussion centered on the problems encountered by public librarians in serving students with large class assignments. The major recommendation agreed on was that public librarians should use the in-service days prior to school opening to speak to teachers of the need for notifying the public librarian in advance of assignments likely to create problems.

Vermont

381. The State of Vermont, Free Public Library Service, is exploring the establishment of a state bibliographic center which will involve all types of libraries.

Wisconsin

382. Association of Beloit Libraries

This is a group of Wisconsin and Illinois libraries of all types in the Beloit area, which meets once a month to discuss cooperative projects. No current projects were reported.

383. Northeast Wisconsin Intertype Libraries (NEWIL)

Representatives of public, college, and school libraries met in 1967 to discuss the feasibility of establishing a cooperative interlibrary project in the Green Bay area. Plans were submitted and approved, funds were received, and the project, with offices at the Brown County Library, Green Bay, was officially initiated in the fall of 1968. A union list of periodicals has been produced, and discussions have centered on methods of joint use, subject coverage, and sharing of audiovisual materials. NEWIL, the first of Wisconsin's "intertype" cooperative projects, involves college, public, university, and school libraries in a common program.

AUTHOR-PROJECT-ORGANIZATION INDEX

This index includes author, cooperative project, and library organization entries. References are to entries in the Annotated Bibliography and Appendix, not page numbers.

Adcock, Elizabeth, 130, 137
Ahlers, Eleanor E., 133
Aiken, Richard S., 313
Allen, Francis W., 36
American Library Assn. Cooperative Cataloging Committee, 1.
Amorim, Maria Jose Theresa de, 124
Anderson, Margaret, 286
Anzalone, Virginia, 204
Ardern, L. L., 77
Area College Library Cooperative Program of Central Pennsylvania (ACLCP), 378
ARLO, see Art Research Libraries of Ohio
Armstrong, Charles M., 30, 63
Art Research Libraries of Ohio (ARLO), 296, 347
Ashworth, Wilfred, 103
Associated Research Materials Center (Yuma, Ariz.), 287
Associated Science Libraries of San Diego, 286, 327
Association of Beloit Libraries, 382
Aurora (Colo.) Library Council, 355
Avins, Wesley, 244

Bailey, Lois, 20
Ball, Alice D., 84
Bard, Harriet E., 140

Bates, Mary, 93
Bauer, Harry, 60
Bebbington, John, 162
Becker, Joseph, 326
Bevis, Dorothy, 262
Bibliographical Center for Research— Rocky Mountain Region, 54, 61, 68, 75, 90, 104, 242, 275
Binns, Norman E., 177
Birkelund, Palle, 141
Black Gold Cooperative Library System (Calif.), 307, 324, 352
Blackshear, Orrilla T., 237
Blasingame, Ralph, 159, 210, 245
Blodgett, Philip R., 91
Bodker, Adele, 204
Bonn, George S., 226
Boord, Miller, 147, 152
Bowron, A. W., 142
Brahm, Walter, 74
Branham, Irene, 23
Brewer, Margaret, 277
British National Bibliography, 181, 240
Brown, H. P., 26
Brown, J. W., 80
Brown, Keith G., 67
Brunette, Margaret, 18
Bryon, J. F. W., 181
Buddington, William S., 327
Burns, Robert W., 323
Burr, Elizabeth, 15, 194, 302

Business and Management Research:
A Guide to the Brooklyn Public
Library Business Library for
Students of Business and
Management, 374
Butler, Joan, 134
Byington, Janice J., 215

California Institute of Technology
Industrial Research Assn., 286
California Library Assn. Regional
Resources Coordinating
Committee, 105
California State Library Processing
Center, 293
California State Union Catalog,
282, 324
Campion, Eleanor Este, 52, 68
Carlson, William H., 10
Carnovsky, Leon, 160
Carruthers, Muriel, 142
Carter, Harriet I., 53, 88
Cataloging in Source, 149
Center for Research Libraries (CRL),
54, 75, 89, 104, 275
Chapman, Eulalia D., 61
Charlotte (N.C.) Area Library
Assn., 263
CICRIS, *see* Cooperative Industrial
and Commercial Reference and
Information Service
Clark, Edward, 66
Collison, R. L. W., 75
Colorado College and Head Librarians
Conference, 4, 5, 6, 13, 90
Commercial and Technical Library
Service, *see* Cooperative Industrial
and Commercial Reference and
Information Service
Committee on Regional Cooperation,
California Library Assn., 72
Conference on School-Public Relations
(N.Y. City), 264
Connor, Jean L., 259
Cooley, Marguerite B., 287
Cooperating Libraries in Consortium
(Minneapolis-St. Paul), 369
Cooperation among Libraries of
Metropolitan New York, 50

Cooperative Acquisitions Project, 54
Cooperative Committee on Library
Buildings, 54
Cooperative Industrial and Commercial
Reference and Information Service
(CICRIS), 100, 120, 146, 167, 177,
187, 231
CORAL, *see* Council of Research
and Academic Libraries
Cory, John M., 328
Costello, Gertrude, 118
Council of Research and Academic
Libraries (CORAL, San Antonio),
272
Crawford, Carolyn, 319
CRL, *see* Center for Research Libraries
Culbertson, Kay, 186
Curley, Walter W., 234
Cuyahoga County (Ohio) Public
Library, 304

Daane, Beth, 216
Dale, N. A., 156
Danish Bibliographical Bureau, 141
David, Charles W., 104
Davis, Winifred, 142
De Soto Trail Regional Library (Ga.),
304
Delaware Rapid Interlibrary Loan
and Reference Service (DRILL),
311, 340
Dennis, Willard K., 69, 193
Denver Bibliographical Center, *see*
Bibliographical Center for Research
—Rocky Mountain Region
Denver Public Library-
Denver Public Schools Council, 304
Directory of Cooperative Library
Activities in New England, 372
Directory of Libraries and Specialized
Collections in the Indianapolis
Metropolitan Area, 360
Directory of Subject Strengths in
Connecticut Libraries, 356
Documents Expediting Project, 54
Downs, Robert B., 21, 207
Drake, Christine, 236
Drennan, Henry T., 157
Drewry, Virginia, 28, 116, 131

DRILL, *see* Delaware Rapid Interlibrary Loan and Reference Service
Dudley, Edward, 146
Dunn, Oliver, 79
Dunningham, A. G. W., 110

East Bay Libraries Council (San Francisco), 40
Eaton, Andrew J., 95
Eckford, Mary Lathrop, 171
Edelman, Hendrik, 246
Edmonds, May, 107
Edson, Miriam M., 123
Edwards, Lon, 111
Electronic Information Sharing Distribution Network (Ga.), 309
Enoch Pratt Free Library, 214
Erie County Public Library, 87
Estabrooks, Edith E., 138
Esterquest, Ralph T., 89, 100, 172
Evanston (Ill.) Public Library, 304

Facsimile Transmissions Experiment (N.Y., FACTS), 264
Fancher, Genevieve, 183
Fancher, Pauline, 183
Farmington Plan, 41, 54, 275
Faulkner-Van Buren Regional Library (Ark.), 151
Ferguson, Elizabeth, 155
First Minnesota Assembly on Inter-library Cooperation, 255
Fischer, Margaret, 275
Folkeboksamlingenes Ekspedisjon, 81
Foltz, Florence P., 29
Forrester, George, 332
Frankenfeld, Mrs. Herbert, 222
Fraser Valley Regional Library (Br. Columbia), 126
Fuller, Helen, 78, 143

Gaines, Ervin J., 329
Galloway, R. Dean, 198
Gardner, Frank M., 187
Gelfand, Morris A., 46
Georgia State Centralized Catalog Card Service, 28, 81, 113, 116, 131
Goldberg, Dorothy, 250
Gosnell, Charles E., 121

Govan, Gilbert E., 3
Grazier, Robert T., 125
Great Britain. Working Party on Inter-library Cooperation in England and Wales, 178
Greater Louisville Technical Referral Center, 363

Haas, Warren J., 205
HADIS, *see* Huddersfield and District Information Scheme
Halvorson, Homer, 8
Hampshire Inter-Library Center, 206
Hancock County (Me.) Library Council, 294
Hanke, Kate G., 109
Hargreaves, Edward, 58
Harm, Melvin P., 309
Harris, Katherine G., 148
Harshe, Florence E., 96
Haugh, W. S., 132
Haviland, Virginia, 19
Hawaii State Centralized Processing Center, 265, 319
Heintze, Ingeborg, 190
Henderson, John D., 31
Hendricks, Donald D., 266
Hennessy, Mildred L., 220
Hertfordshire Technical Library and Information Service, 177
Hildebrand, Lorraine, 313
Hill, Andrew P., 32
Hill, Laurence G., 250
Hirsch, Rudolph, 104
Hodgson, James G., 13, 90
Hoeffgen, Helen, 333
Holden, Edna, 24
Holley, Edward G., 266
Holt, Raymond M., 307
Homeyer, B. C., 99
Hopkinson, Shirley L., 173
Horn, William A., 261
Horsley, Lucile, 180
Hoskin, Beryl, 175
Houston List of Scientific and Technical Serial Publications, 196, 202, 286
Houston Technical Information Center, 196

Houze, Robert A., 272
Howard, Edward N., 334
Hubbard, C. S., 12
Huddersfield and District Information Scheme (HADIS), 167, 231
Hughesdon, Harold, 118
Hull Technical Interloan Scheme (HULTIS), 177, 231
Humphry, John A., 191, 206, 308
Hunt, K. G., 101

Indiana Communication System, 248
Individualized Learning Center (West Concord, Mass.), 367
Industrial Information Service (IIS, Southern Methodist Univ.), 266
Industrial Research Service (Detroit), 33
Interlibrary Center, Univ. of North Carolina, 276
Interlibrary Loan by Publisher Plan, 254

Jackson, William V., 135
Jefferson, George, 227
Joeckel, Carleton B., 14, 31, 32, 33
Joint Committee of the National Education Assn. and the American Library Assn., 2
Joint Committee on Cooperation with Schools, 17
Josey, E. J., 254, 264
Josselyn, Clara, 78

Kaczmarek, Carol, 238
Kaser, David, 176
Kerr, G., 22
Kingery, Robert E., 163
Klitzke, Lewis W., 195
Krarup, Agnes, 59
Kroll, Morton, 157
Kuhlman, August F., 7, 20, 35
Kusel, Mary A., 114
Kyle, Barbara, 58

LACAP, *see* Latin American Cooperative Acquisitions Project
LADSIRLAC, *see* Liverpool and District Scientific Industrial and Research Libraries Advisory Council

Lagos (Nigeria) Special Libraries Information Service (LASLIS), 349
Lamb, J. P., 44, 102
Latin American Cooperative Acquisitions Project (LACAP), 163, 165
Laursen, Johs. Lehm., 273
Leonard, Virginia, 241
Lewis, Helen B., 47
Lewiston-Auburn (Me.) Twin Cities Library Council, 294
Ley, Ronald, 126
Libraries and Specialized Collections in the Vigo County (Ind.) Area, 361
Library Group of Southwestern Connecticut, 199, 233
Library Network Directors' Group, 350
Library of Congress Mission for Cooperative Acquisition, 41
Library Service Center of Eastern Ohio, 171
Lightfoot, Robert M., Jr., 348
Lindauer, Dinah S., 213, 235
Linderman, Winifred B., 248
List of Serials in Chicago, 275
Little, Arthur D., Inc., 247
Little, Robert, 238
Liverpool and District Scientific Industrial and Research Libraries Advisory Council (LADSIRLAC), 167, 177, 231
Longworth, Ruth O., 97
Lorenz, John G., 248
Losinski, Julia, 239

McAnally, Arthur M., 54
McClaskey, Harris C., 219, 258
McColvin, Lionel R., 76
McDiarmid, E. W., 30
MacDonald, Mary Jane, 279
McIntyre, John P., 217
McJenkin, Virginia, 230
Mahoney, Orcena, 113
Mahoney, R. E., 65
Malek, Rudolf, 189
Manchester Technical Information Service (MANTIS), 231
Marland, Sidney P., 161
Martin, Gene, 224

Martin, Lowell A., 314
Mason, Diana, 298
Mason, H. J., 289
Mecklenburg (N.C.) Library Assn., 263
Memphis Librarians' Committee, 229
Merritt, Bernice, 201
Metcalf, Keyes D., 48, 98, 158, 170
METRO, see New York Metropolitan Reference and Research Library Agency, Inc.
Metropolitan Library Council of Chicago, 14
Metropolitan Library Service Agency (Minneapolis-St. Paul), 255
Midwest Inter-Library Center, see Center for Research Libraries
Might, Mamie, 16
MILC, see Center for Research Libraries
Minder, Thomas, 338
Minnesota Interlibrary Teletype Experiment (MINITEX), 274, 346
Missoula (Mont.) Area Library Club, 325, 370
Missouri Libraries Planning Committee, 95
M.I.T. Industrial Liaison Program, 286
Montclair (N.J.) School and Public Library Relations Committee (SPLARC), 230
Moore, Helen-Jean, 184
Morchand, Charles A., 249
Morchand Transmission System, 249
Morison, C. K., 142
Morsch, Lucile M., 81
Mountain-Plains Library Assn., 90
Murdock, Faith T., 305
Murphy, Virginia B., 268
Murray, Tom, 252
Myers, Walter E., 38

Nassau County Library Assn., 9
Nassau (N.Y.) Library System, 213, 235, 259, 261, 300
National Committee on Regional Library Cooperation (Gr. Brit.), 43, 64
National Film Board (Canada), 26
National Film Society (Canada), 22, 26
National Lending Library for Science and Technology (N.L.L., England), 168
National Union Catalog, 275
Neff, Evaline B., 344
Nelson Associates, Inc., 211, 269, 290, 315, 316
NELTAS, see Northeast Lancashire Technical Advisory Service
NEPBC, see Northeastern Pennsylvania Bibliographic Center
Ness, Charles H., 280
New England Deposit Library, 98, 108, 275
New Jersey Joint Committee on Cooperation with Schools, 17
New Jersey Referral Center, 289
New Mexico State Library Demonstration Traveling Library Center, 373
New York Metropolitan Reference and Research Library Agency, Inc. (METRO), 25, 246, 249, 253, 270, 308, 328
New York State Interlibrary Loan Pilot Project (NYSILL), 264, 290, 315
Newhouse, Jeanne, 119
NEWIL, see Northeast Wisconsin Intertype Libraries
Nioga (N.Y.) Library System, 250, 259, 261, 305
Nolting, Orin F., 317
North Carolina Research Triangle, 289
North Carolina Union Catalog, 128, 276
North Texas Regional Libraries, 7, 20
North-Western Regional Library Bureau (England), 77
Northeast Lancashire Technical Advisory Service (NELTAS), 231
Northeast Wisconsin Intertype Libraries (NEWIL), 383
Northeastern Pennsylvania Bibliographic Center (NEPBC), 379
Northeastern Regional Library, 48, 49
Northern Great Plains Library Planning Council, 90
Northwestern Regional Library (N.W. Ontario), 122
Nott, Julie H., 251
NYSILL, see New York State Interlibrary Loan Pilot Project

O'Keefe, Richard L., 202
Omaha Union Catalog of Chemistry Information, 125
Orne, Jerrold, 276
Orr, Marion, 82
Orvig, Mary, 55
Otternik, Gosta, 200

Pacific Northwest Bibliographic Center, 11, 33, 60, 68, 91, 104, 275
Pacific Northwest Federation of Forestry Libraries, 323
Pacific Northwest Library Assn., 10
Pacific Northwest Library Assn. Library Development Project, 117, 157
Parrott, F. P., 150
Parsons, Arthur H., Jr., 303
Paulin, L. V., 167
Pearson, Wilfred, 58
Pennsylvania Technical Assistance Program (PENNTAP), 345
Pfoutz, Daniel R., 345
Phelps, Rose B., 135
Philadelphia Bibliographical Center and Union Library Catalog, 52, 75, 125, 186
Philadelphia Metropolitan Library Council, 14
Phillips, Janet, 135
Phipps, Mildred R., 144
Pike, Eugene, 282
Poindron, P., 188
Pooler, Jack, 208
Pottinger, M. C., 41
Prince George's County (Md.), 305
Prince George's County (Md.) Memorial Library, 261
Purdy, G. Flint, 330

Rates, R. D., 120
Regional Council for Education in the South, 54
Regional Information and Communication Exchange (RICE, Houston), 233, 266, 267, 286, 320
Regional Planning Committee of the New England Library Assn., 372
Regional Reference and Research Library Program (N.Y.), 248

Reynolds, Michael M., 185
Richards, John S., 11
Richardson, Harold G., 196
River Bend Library System (Moline, Ill.), 318
Roberts Report, 136, 178
Rochester Regional Research Library Council, 344
Rocky Mountain Bibliographical Center, *see* Bibliographical Center for Research—Rocky Mountain Region
Roedde, W. A., 122
Rowell, Adelaide C., 3

Sacramento Area Library Organization (SALO), 354
Salt Lake County Library System, 304
Sampley, Arthur M., 35
Sams, Mrs. Arch., 83
San Antonio Area Specialized Library Resources, 272
Sass, Samuel, 145
Scarborough Information Network (SIN), 298, 332
Schenk, Gretchen K., 30, 87
Science Service Library Network, 226
Scurfield, Jannetta G., 45
Selby, Mildred, 106
Servicio de Intercambio de Catalogacao (SIC), 81, 124
Sewell, P. H., 43
Shank, Russell, 270, 320
Shared Acquisitions and Retention System (SHARES), 246
Sharp, Harold S., 145
Sheffield (England) Interchange Organization (SINTO), 44, 102, 162, 167, 177, 187, 231
Shepard, Martha, 283
Sheridan, Robert N., 260
Sherwood, Janice W., 68
Shuman, Bruce A., 342
SIC, *see* Servicio de Intercambio de Catalogacao
Silvester, Elizabeth, 228
SIN, *see* Scarborough Information Network
SINTO, *see* Sheffield (England) Interchange Organization

148

Sisson, Jacqueline D., 296, 347
Skipper, James E., 158
Smith, Bernice S., 10
Smith, Hannis S., 154, 179, 255
Southeastern New York Library Resources Council, 339, 376
Southern Illinois Regional Library, 152
Southern Oregon Library Federation, 285, 299
Southwest Regional Library (Mo.), 193
SPLARC, see Montclair (N.J.) School and Public Library Relations Committee
Stanford, Edward B., 127, 274
State Technical Services Act of 1965, 289
Stavely, Ronald, 39
Stevens, Frank A., 218
Stevens, Janet R. T., 214
Suffolk (N.Y.) Library System, 234, 259
Swank, R. C., 242

Tacoma (Wash.) Area Urban Coalition Education Task Force, 313
TALIC, see Tyneside Association of Libraries for Industry and Commerce
Tauber, Maurice F., 108
Taylor, Frank R., 231
Taylor, Helene Scherff, 139
Taylor, Kenneth I., 237
Taylor, Mark, 166
Technical Information Service (TIS, Stanford Univ.), 208
Technical Services Center (Tucson), 287
Texas Information Exchange (TIE), 267
Thomassen, Cora E., 319, 320, 321, 222
TIE, see Texas Information Exchange
TIS, see Technical Information Service
Tolman, Mason, 129
Trotier, Arnold H., 149
Tucker, Harold W., 220
Tucson (Ariz.) Area Library Council, 271
Turgason, Anna J., 51
Tyneside Association of Libraries for Industry and Commerce (TALIC), 167, 177, 187, 231

Union Catalog of Northeastern Pennsylvania, 275

Union Catalog of Pennsylvania, 280
United States Book Exchange (USBE), 54, 84, 92
University-Industry Research Program (UIR, Univ. of Wis.), 252
University of Washington Film Center, 80
Uridge, Margaret D., 40
Urquhart, D. J., 168

Vamberry, Joseph T., 257
Van Deusen, Neil C., 30
Van Riemsdijk, G. A., 197
Vann, Sarah K., 321
Vedder, Agnes B., 30
Vermont, State Bibliographic Center, 381
Vollans, Robert F., 64
Vormelker, Rose L., 289

Walford, A. J., 58
Wallis, C. Lamar, 229
Wand, M. W., 112
Warner, Gilmore, 94
Waterville (Me.) Area Council, 294
Watts, Doris Ryder, 119
Wayne County (Mich.) Federated Library System, 284, 316
Weber, David C., 208
Wells, A. J., 256
Wemmer, Frederick, 105
Wenberg, Louise T., 157
Westchester (N.Y.) Library System, 225, 239, 259, 261, 305
Western Regional Public Library System (Mass.), 206
Wezeman, Frederick, 221
Wheeler, Marjorie, 251
White, Carl M., 49
White, Ruth M., 192
Whittier (Calif.) Area Library Study Committee, 212
Wickersham, Lucille, 191
Wiese, Bernice, 62
Willett, Mary A., 57
Williams, Edwin E., 92
Wilson, Louis Round, 108
Winkler, Loretta M., 232, 239
Winnick, Pauline, 261

Winslow, Amy, 14
Wisconsin Resource Interlace, 302
Wood, Susanna B., 37
Woods, Bill M., 233
Wright, Donald E., 322

Yakima Valley Regional Library, 243
Year's Work in Librarianship, The, 34
Yungmeyer, Elinor, 223

Zimmerman, Carma R., 33

TYPES OF COOPERATIVE ACTIVITY
INDEX

The main categories in this index are based on Purdy's classification of cooperative library activities. The subdivisions in some of the categories also are adaptations of Purdy's scheme.* Although the final date in these lists is given as 1968, some items from 1969 are included.

References are to entry numbers in the Annotated Bibliography and the Appendix, not to pages.

Union Lists, Union Catalogs, and Bibliographic Centers

DATE	UNION LISTS	UNION CATALOGS	BIBLIOGRAPHICAL CENTERS
1940–44	None	3 8 9	10 11
1945–49	13 35	None	13 33
1950–54	58 79 85	43 68 79 45 70 85 64 71 94	52 61 91 54 75 60 90
1955–59	103 120 135 110 125 118 129	100 125 136 108 128 145 112 135	104 145
1960–64	162 196 208 167 199 187 202	159 177 190 162 184 167 186	174
1965–68	211 254 287 229 263 312 243 268 313 244 275 327 252 286 334	211 280 332 215 282 238 283 275 306 276 324	242 275
Appendix	352 361 378 356 363 379 357 366 383 360 376	None	381

*G. Flint Purdy, "Interrelations among Public, School, and Academic Libraries," *Library Quarterly* 39: 52-63 (Jan. 1969).

Cooperative Development of Resources

DATE				
1940–44	3 10 11			
1945–49	23 36	41 42		
1950–54	54 75	85 89		
1955–59	100 101 103	104 108 118	120 125 148	153
1960–64	160 163 164	165 176 181	184 186 188	189 198
1965–68	238 243 254	275 276 286	296 323 327	332 347
Appendix	369 375	378 379		

Sharing Resources

Three categories of sharing resources in terms of use are listed. The first is areawide access based on networks of libraries, whether in a metropolitan area, on a statewide basis, or in regions which include more than one state. The second involves the public use of academic, special, or school libraries under limited access agreements; the third lists instances of the public library being used by people whose primary outlet is an academic, school, or special library. "Resources" is interpreted broadly to include reference service, staff, physical facilities, as well as print and nonprint resources.

Sharing Resources (contd.)

DATE	AREAWIDE ACCESS NETWORKS			PUBLIC USE OF ACADEMIC, SPECIAL, OR SCHOOL LIBRARIES		USE OF PUBLIC LIBRARY BY SPECIAL OR SCHOOL LIBRARY PATRONS		
1940–44	9			3		2 3		
1945–49	22 26			27		15 16 18	24 29 31	32 33 37
1950–54	43 45 54 60 61 64	68 70 71 73 75 76	80 87 91 92 94	47 51 54 55 57	63 69 93 96	44 47 51 54 55	57 62 63 69 74	77 83 95
1955–59	100 101 104 108 110 121 122	125 128 136 141 146 152		112 114 147 152 155		100 102 106 109 111 112 114	119 120 123 126 132 134 137	143 144 146 155 156
1960–64	159 189 190 196	200 205		175 180 193 208		162 167 175 177	183 186 187 193	195 201
1965–68	248 253 259 264 267 273 274 275 279 280 281 282	285 286 288 289 290 295 296 297 298 311 315 326	327 328 332 334 336 337 338 340 344 346	216 236 251 252 254 274 286 289 329		216 217 218 219 220 222 229 231 239 250 259 260	261 288 292 303 305 307 310 329 335 341 348	
Appendix	350 363 369	376 378		349 362 368		352 353 364	365 367 371	375

153

Communication

This area of cooperative activity is subdivided into three categories. The first is formal organizations and includes established and continuing bodies which meet regularly for discussion of mutual problems, cooperative planning, and decision-making. The second category includes such informal arrangements as joint communities, irregular meetings, ad hoc groups, and informal personal contact. The third is networks which includes teletype, telephone, computer, and facsimile transmission networks.

DATE	FORMAL ORGANIZATIONS	INFORMAL ARRANGEMENTS	NETWORKS
1940–44	13	None	None
1945–49	18 40	19	None
1950–54	None	78 93	None
1955–59	None	115	None
1960–64	190 199	166 201 182	None
1965–68	214 285 344 230 286 232 294 256 304 259 305 261 325 271 339	222 225 237 238 231 343	248 297 327 253 298 332 259 301 340 267 308 342 274 309 346 281 311 286 320
Appendix	350 355 382 354 370	380	358 379 363

154

Centralized Processing

DATE					
1940–44	1 4	5 6			
1945–49	12 18	28			
1950–54	55 59	66 81	97		
1955–59	107 113 114	116 124 130	131 137 140	141 149	
1960–64	171 173	200			
1965–68	238 240 256	259 265 273	276 284 288	293 304 318	319 321 324
Appendix	351				

Cooperative Plans and Surveys

The second category listed below is an extremely broad one and could possibly include all the examples of cooperative activity. An attempt has been made here to restrict it to examples where cooperative planning is conducted on a continuing basis within the framework of established committees or groups.

DATE	SURVEYS OF RESOURCES AND NEEDS	COOPERATIVE PLANNING
1940–44	7	None
1945–49	20 30 21 40	14 25 17 36
1950–54	48 64 95 49 91	46 86 50
1955–59	105 128 117 136	118
1960–64	157 170 191 158 178 194 168 185 207	203
1965–68	210 235 266 315 211 242 270 316 226 245 272 228 247 290 232 262 314	212 246 296 338 213 249 299 344 224 255 302 238 285 308 239 295 323
Appendix	None	351 355 372 382

Cooperative Storage

DATE				
1940–44	None			
1945–49	None			
1950–54	48 49	50 57	72 75	98
1955–59	108	118		
1960–64	None			
1965–68	275			
Appendix	369			

Cooperative Computer Center

DATE	
1940–44	None
1945–49	None
1950–54	None
1955–59	None
1960–64	None
1965–69	None
Appendix	363

TYPES OF LIBRARY COOPERATION INDEX*

References are to entry numbers in the Annotated Bibliography and the Appendix.

DATE	ACADEMIC SCHOOL PUBLIC SPECIAL	ACADEMIC PUBLIC SPECIAL	ACADEMIC SCHOOL PUBLIC	ACADEMIC SCHOOL SPECIAL	PUBLIC SCHOOL SPECIAL
1940–44	1	None	3	None	None
1945–49	14 33 21	None	30	None	None
1950–54	46 84 53 91 60 92 81 95	45 64 50 71 52	None	None	None
1955–59	105 129 117 135 124 141 125 149 128	100 110 101 118 104 121 108	151	None	None
1960–64	159 190 172 205 189 207	162 196 167 199 177	175 191 204	None	None
**1965–68	210 224 247 254 255 269 271 302 314 316 325 326 338	229 287 231 290 233 295 246 296 248 297 249 298 253 308 255 312 259 315 266 320 267 323 268 327 270 328 275 336 276 337 283 344 286 347	216 285 330 332	None	244
Appendix	350 372 356 377 361 381 370 382	352 363 357 366 359 379 360	383	None	355 365

*The category of School-Public Libraries is omitted because of the unusually large number of items in that category.

Types of Library Cooperation Index (contd.)

ACADEMIC PUBLIC		ACADEMIC SCHOOL	ACADEMIC SPECIAL	PUBLIC SPECIAL		SCHOOL SPECIAL
3	6	None	None	3		None
4	7					
5	9					
13	27	None	None	33		None
20	35					
26	41					
73	94	None	58	44		None
80	99		75	67		
93			77	76		
101	148	None	104	102	120	None
113	152		125	103	146	
125	153		127	104	155	
147				112		
170	186	None	185	None		None
176	187		202			
179	188		203			
180	197		208			
184	206					
236	307	None	233	219		286
242	309		245	258		
253	310		251	308		
254	311		252	316		
273	318		272	318		
274	324		286	324		
275	339			334		
279	340					
280	342					
293	343					
301	346					
306	348					
352	374	362	349	None		None
358	376	368				
371	378					

**Although the final date is given as 1968, some items from 1969 are included.